MESSAGE:

_____

_____

_____

*I thank my God, making mention
of you always in my prayers.*
~ PHILEMON 4

hed by Christian Art Publishers
ox 1599, Vereeniging, 1930, RSA

_022

First edition 2022

Designed by Christian Art Publishers

Cover designed by Christian Art Publishers
Images used under license from Shutterstock.com

Some quotations taken from *Gathered Gold: A Treasury of Quotations for Christians* by John Blanchard.

Unless otherwise indicated, all Scripture quotations
are taken from the New King James Version®.
Copyright © 1979, 1980, 1982 by Thomas Nelson, Inc.
Used by permission. All rights reserved.

Scripture quotations marked NLT are taken from
the Holy Bible, *New Living Translation*,
copyright © 1996, 2004, 2015 by Tyndale House Foundation.
Used by permission of Tyndale House Publishers,
Carol Stream, Illinois 60188.
All rights reserved.

Printed in China

ISBN 978-1-77637-114-3

23  24  25  26  27  28  29  30  31  32  –  11  10  9  8  7  6  5  4  3  2

# POCKET PRAYERS
## FOR EVERY DAY

## ANGUS BUCHAN

CHRISTIAN ART
PUBLISHERS

I really want to thank our Lord Jesus
for two of my special daughters,
Robyn Maclean and Jilly Hull,
who have been instrumental in
helping me with this,
my very first book of prayer.

I also want to thank our Lord Jesus
for their continued support from
the outset of my passion for writing.
They have been a tremendous
inspiration and comfort to me in
many times of trial and tribulation.

*I would like to dedicate this
beautiful prayer devotional
to my dear wife and best friend, Jill.*

*Not only is she the mother of my children
and the granny of our grandchildren,
but she is also my personal intercessor.*

*She is the one who stands in the gap for
me all the time. When I am away, my
eyes fill with tears when she prays for
me over the phone. Jill has taught me
so much about praying and spending
time in the presence of God.*

*I am so grateful that we
serve our Lord Jesus together.
In fact, I can tell you honestly,
without her prayers, I would never be
able to do the work Jesus has called me to.*

# CONTENTS

# JANUARY

*All to Jesus I Surrender*

# A LIVING SACRIFICE

*Zacchaeus said, "Look, Lord, I give half of my goods to the poor; and if I have taken anything from anyone by false accusation, I restore fourfold."*

~ LUKE 19:8

Lord Jesus, the sheer joy of giving the best I have to the One I love the most is the true meaning of the word *sacrifice!* Just like Zacchaeus, because You have rescued me from sure death, both physically and spiritually, everything I have I desire to give to You! This new year, take my life and let it be a living sacrifice to You alone.

 *Amen.*

*Take my life and let it be consecrated, Lord, to Thee.*
– Francis R. Havergal

# GOD WILL DELIVER YOU

*Many are the afflictions of the righteous, but the* LORD *delivers him out of them all.*

~ PSALM 34:19

Sweet Jesus, sometimes I wonder
why so many of Your children
suffer so much. Then I realize that
we live in a fallen world where the
devil and his demons operate.
We are not exempt from trials and
tribulations. However, the wonderful
reassuring good news is that
You deliver us out of all of them.

— *Amen.* —

*The fiery trials of life only purify*
*us for eternity with Jesus.*

# FOLLOW AFTER THE MASTER

*Then He said to them all, "If anyone desires to come after Me, let him deny himself, and take up his cross daily, and follow Me."*

~ LUKE 9:23

Dear Jesus, it is not easy to put the flesh down, for it continues to raise its ugly head. Please help me, Holy Spirit, to rather focus and concentrate on heavenly things, instead of the cheap plastic things of this earthly life. Help me to rather emulate and follow after the examples of men like Jim Elliot who sacrificed his life at 28 years of age while boldly and fearlessly preaching the gospel.

*Amen.*

*He is no fool who gives what he cannot keep to gain what he cannot lose.*
– Jim Elliot

# ALL OF HIM, NONE OF ME

*Now a certain ruler asked Him, saying, "Good Teacher, what shall I do to inherit eternal life?"*

~ LUKE 18:18

Dearest heavenly Father, I am so well aware of the absolute shortcomings in my life with You. Like the ruler who thought he was doing so well and yet was still so full of self, I too feel like that sometimes. Please inspire my heart to sing that old hymn once again, "None of self and all of Thee." Help me to surrender all to You.

— *Amen.* —

*All of self, and none of Thee. Some of self, and some of Thee. Less of self, and more of Thee. None of self, and all of Thee.*

– Théodore Monod

# LAYING DOWN YOUR LIFE

*"For God so loved the world that He gave His only begotten Son, that whoever believes in Him should not perish but have everlasting life."*

~ JOHN 3:16

Father God, You loved the world so much that You sacrificed Your only begotten Son. That is why I love and respect You so very much! You always lead by example, always leading from the front. You don't sit comfortably in some ivory tower directing operations. No, You sacrificed Your only Son for a sinner like me. Thank You, Father!

— *Amen.* —

*I have now concentrated all my prayers into one, and that one prayer is this, that I may die to self, and live wholly to Him.*
– Charles Spurgeon

# NO GREATER LOVE

*"There is no greater love than to lay down one's life for one's friends."*

~ JOHN 15:13 NLT

My dear Lord Jesus, You have given me so very much. In fact, if it were not for You and for dying in my place on that old rugged cross, I do not know where I would have been today. So, I want to say quite simply and humbly, thank You for giving up Your life so that I can obtain eternal life.

— *Amen.* —

*In that old rugged cross, stained with blood so divine, a wondrous beauty I see, for 'twas on that old cross Jesus suffered and died, to pardon and sanctify me.*
– George Bennard

# DISCIPLINING YOUR BODY

*I discipline my body and bring it into subjection.*
~ 1 CORINTHIANS 9:27

Father God, as a Christian, undoubtedly one of the hardest sacrifices I have to make is to discipline my earthly body and bring it in line with Your holy Scriptures. Otherwise, I could become a terrible stumbling block to others. Please help me to be a good example to the world, and to not conform to sloppy and even sinful standards.

*Amen.*

*Discipline, for the Christian, begins with the body. It is this body that is the primary material given to us for sacrifice.*
– Elisabeth Elliot

# DYING TO LIVE

*"Most assuredly, I say to you, unless a grain of wheat falls into the ground and dies, it remains alone; but if it dies, it produces much grain."*

~ JOHN 12:24

Father God, I realize that unless I am prepared to completely die to self, You cannot use me. I ask, Holy Spirit, that today You will take from me all self-centeredness and selfishness, and fill me with the undiluted love of Jesus. May I always see others better than myself. It is in dying to self that we truly start to live.

 *Amen.*

*When Christ calls a man,*
*He bids him come and die.*
– Dietrich Bonhoeffer

# SERVING DILIGENTLY

*"For whoever desires to save his life will lose it, but whoever loses his life for My sake and the gospel's will save it."*

~ MARK 8:35

Master, when I think of what Your disciples gave up for Your sake – their homes, families, dreams – I realize that I have surrendered very little in comparison. Show me, please, the areas I need to hand over in order to serve You more diligently and effectively, I pray.

— *Amen.* —

*A faith that has cost us nothing is worth nothing.*

# WHOLEHEARTED OBEDIENCE

*As for me and my family, we will serve the Lord.*
*~ Joshua 24:15 NLT*

Dearest Lord Jesus, I ask You today
to please impress upon me the
importance of never denying Your
name or ever compromising Your
holy written Word for any person
or any worldly ambition. Not to
serve any foreign gods, but only
You, the true King of all kings.

 *Amen.*

*The end product of sacrifice is*
*to obey God's holy written Word.*

# BOUGHT AT A PRICE

*For you were bought at a price.*

*~ 1 CORINTHIANS 6:20*

Dear Father God, in comparison with the gigantic sacrifice that Your Son, Jesus, made for me on Calvary, I agree completely with the words of David Livingstone when he said that he had never made a sacrifice at all, even spending himself until death preaching the gospel in Africa. Thank You for paying the greatest price to save me.

*Amen.*

*People talk of the sacrifice I have made in spending so much of my life in Africa. Can that be called a sacrifice which is simply paid back as a small part of a great debt owing to our God, which we can never repay?*
– David Livingstone

# A TRUE SACRIFICE

*"Simon, son of Jonah, do you love Me more than these?"*

~ JOHN 21:15

Father God, the measure of my love for You is determined by the scale of how much I am prepared to sacrifice for You. Father, please guide me in giving up any passions that I might have that keep me from serving You. Help me to make a true sacrifice so that I can use all of my time telling lost souls where to find the way through Jesus, Your Son. Holy Spirit, please do not allow me to lose sight of my first love (see Revelation 2:4).

— *Amen.* —

*Our attitude (sacrifice)
determines our altitude for God.*

# NEVER IN NEED

*And my God shall supply all your need according to His riches in glory by Christ Jesus.*

~ PHILIPPIANS 4:19

Dearest Father in heaven, I love You so much. Not only are You my Father, but You're also my Provider. Please forgive me for so often becoming anxious. There is absolutely no cause whatsoever for me to be so. Not once in my entire life have You ever deserted me. Your Word promises that You will meet all my needs. For this I praise You.

— *Amen.* —

*We can never "out bless" the Lord.*

# SURRENDERED TO CHRIST

*For to me, to live is Christ, and to die is gain.*
~ PHILIPPIANS 1:21

Lord Jesus, what a powerful statement
Paul makes here. It reveals total
and complete sacrifice, but what
incredible joy and peace comes
with a heart completely sacrificed
to You! And that is the reason
Paul was used so powerfully in the
preaching of the gospel. Holy Spirit,
help me, I pray, to die more to self
each day and to live more for Jesus.

—— *Amen.* ——

*God is looking for some wicks to burn.*
*The oil and the fire are free.*
– James Hudson Taylor

# WALK THE EXTRA MILE

*Do not forget to entertain strangers, for by so doing some have unwittingly entertained angels.*

~ HEBREWS 13:2

Father God, please help me to be much more sympathetic towards strangers; to treat them with much love and respect. Yes, to go the extra mile for them because I might very well be entertaining angels. Help me never to judge others on outward appearance but rather through the eyes of love and acceptance.

*Amen.*

*Never ever judge a book by its cover.*

# ABRAHAM'S OBEDIENCE

*"Offer him there as a burnt offering on one of the mountains."*

~ GENESIS 22:2

Dear Master, now this is an absolutely massive sacrifice. Abraham waited for twenty-five years for his son, Isaac, and then You tested Abraham's obedience by asking him to sacrifice his son. The miracle was that Abraham never hesitated. No wonder You loved him so much. Please help me to obey You, whatever the cost.

*Amen.*

*God says it; I believe it; and that settles it!*
– Smith Wigglesworth

# A FOOL FOR JESUS

*"Go into all the world and preach the gospel to every creature."*

~ MARK 16:15

Lord God, it is no easy task
preaching Your Holy Word.
But I am more than prepared to
give up my reputation in order to be
obedient to Your call to all believers.
God, help me to be a fool for Jesus
and not to think too highly of myself.

*Amen.*

*The Great Commission is not an option to be considered; it is a command to be obeyed.*
– James Hudson Taylor

# TRUE MERCY AND LOVE

*"For I desire mercy and not sacrifice, and the knowledge of God more than burnt offerings."*

~ HOSEA 6:6

Father, You require true sacrifice from me, not just a superficial show of religion. You desire mercy from me and I believe this means that I am to put my brother before myself. It can be very hard at times, especially when he repeatedly lets me down or takes advantage of my mercy. But then again, for his sake, tough love is required. Please help me to genuinely love others as You have loved me.

*Amen.*

*True mercy and love sometimes mean to correct and discipline a person.*

# TIME TO BE STILL

*"Be still, and know that I am God!"*

~ Psalm 46:10 NLT

Father God, I want to ask You
to please forgive me for so
often feeling that I am making a
sacrifice when I take time to be
still and to know that You are God.
It should not be so; it should be a
tremendous honor and privilege
to be quiet and sit at Your feet.

 *Amen.*

*To have God speak to the heart is a majestic
experience, an experience that people may
miss if they monopolize the conversation
and never pause to hear God's responses.*

– Charles Stanley

# BLESSED TO BE A BLESSING

*"Assuredly, I say to you, inasmuch as you did it to one of the least of these My brethren, you did it to Me."*

~ MATTHEW 25:40

Father, it is quite impossible to out bless You and the more we try to sacrifice by giving to the widow and the orphan (see James 1:27), the more You give to us in so many different ways. Thank You for blessing me and my family so abundantly.

— *Amen.* —

*God will be our compensation*
*for every sacrifice we have made.*
– F. B. Meyer

# ALIVE IN CHRIST JESUS

*Reckon yourselves to be dead indeed to sin, but alive to God in Christ Jesus our Lord.*

~ ROMANS 6:11

My dearest Lord Jesus, today I am reminded yet once more that dying to self is no real sacrifice at all. In fact, my biggest drawback is myself and my inclination to sin. When I die to self, that is when I really start to live. Thank You, Master, for showing me the way to abundant life. Thank You for forgiving my sins.

— *Amen.* —

*What a beautiful paradox – it's in dying that we really start to live.*

# LOUDER THAN WORDS

*Obedience is better than sacrifice, and submission is better than offering the fat of rams.*

~ 1 SAMUEL 15:22 NLT

Heavenly Father, thank You for
reminding me yet again that
actions speak louder than words.
You require obedience rather than
empty words and still no change.
Holy Spirit, please help me to be
one who takes action rather than
one who makes empty promises.
I want to follow through with my
obedience to You. I need to walk the
talk and show You that I love You.

 *Amen.*

*We must not keep telling God that we love
Him, but rather show Him that we love Him.*

# TRUE SACRIFICE

*"I have glorified You on the earth. I have finished the work which You have given Me to do."*

~ JOHN 17:4

Lord Jesus, You left Your home in glory to come down to earth to save a wretch like me. What an incredible sacrifice You have made. Thank You, Lord. Please forgive me when I complain about doing Your work. The sacrifices I make for You are nothing compared to the Greatest Sacrifice of all.

*Amen.*

*True sacrifice is giving up something precious for others when they cannot repay you.*

# BY HIS STRIPES WE ARE HEALED

*But He was wounded for our transgressions, He was bruised for our iniquities; the chastisement for our peace was upon Him, and by His stripes we are healed.*

~ ISAIAH 53:5

My dearest Lord Jesus, I want to thank You for taking the whipping on Your back for my healing. Please help us remember to take that promise made for each and every one of us by faith in Your written Word. You paid a terrible price for our healing, let us never take it for granted.

— *Amen.* —

*If Jesus Christ be God and died for me, then no sacrifice can be too great for me to make for Him.*
– C. T. Studd

# FOR HIS SAKE

*"For whoever desires to save his life will lose it, but whoever loses his life for My sake and the gospel's will save it."*

~ MARK 8:35

Father God, I realize it is only in giving that I shall receive and in dying that I shall truly live. Please help me to die to this flesh, to sacrifice the fleshly desire daily so that I can really start to live in the fullness of all that You have prepared for me in this life. You still have so much for me to accomplish for You!

— *Amen.* —

*Self-preservation limits the faith journey Jesus has prepared for those who love Him.*

# A MUSTARD SEED OF FAITH

*"If you have faith as a mustard seed, you will say to this mountain, 'Move from here to there,' and it will move; and nothing will be impossible for you."*
~ MATTHEW 17:20

Father God, I realize that You must often be disappointed by my lack of faith. I look at my own limitations instead of trusting in You. Please increase my faith – even if just by a mustard seed – and keep me focused on who You are and not on what I can do by myself.

*Amen.*

*The reason birds can fly and we can't is simply because they have perfect faith, for to have faith is to have wings.*
– J. M. Barrie

# SERVING HIM ALONE

*"No one can serve two masters; for either he will hate the one and love the other, or else he will be loyal to the one and despise the other. You cannot serve God and mammon."*

~ MATTHEW 6:24

Lord Jesus, these are strong words spoken by You and I know that a real sacrifice is needed on my part to stick to the undiluted principles of the Holy Bible. I must not deviate from it to the left or to the right, then I will know that the Holy Spirit will undertake for me in all my needs. Please help me in this, Lord.

*Amen.*

*We can't expect to hunt with the hounds and run with the hares.*

# YOU REAP WHAT YOU SOW

*But this I say: He who sows sparingly will also reap sparingly, and he who sows bountifully will also reap bountifully.*

~ 2 Corinthians 9:6

Father God, when we look at a farmer
and his crops, we understand the
sowing and reaping principle very well.
There is always a great sacrifice
required by faith when planting
because if we don't put it all in,
then we can't expect a bountiful result.
This applies to every area of life.
Please help me to give it all for You.

— *Amen.* —

*If you plant nothing,
you will surely harvest nothing.*

# LIVING A HOLY LIFE

*May the God of peace Himself sanctify you completely.*

~ 1 THESSALONIANS 5:23

Father God, please sanctify me
through the power of Your Holy Spirit,
our Helper, because I really want
to live a holy life pleasing to You.
I cannot do it alone, but I am
prepared to make the sacrifice so
that I can know and please You
more every day of my life on earth.
— *Amen.* —

*Holiness is the end product of obedience.*

# A LIFETIME OF OBEDIENCE

*Rejoicing in hope, patient in tribulation, continuing steadfastly in prayer.*

~ ROMANS 12:12

Father, this beautiful Scripture speaks to me very clearly about one thing and that is *discipline*. It is not a once-off commitment; it is rather a lifestyle that takes extreme personal sacrifice to fulfill. Please help me daily to be obedient to You in Bible reading and prayer, and to wait on You in the midst of trials and uncertainties, knowing that You are shaping me through them.

*Amen.*

*The making of a man or woman of God is not completed in a moment, it takes a lifetime.*

# FINISHING STRONG

*"For which of you, intending to build a tower, does not sit down first and count the cost, whether he has enough to finish it."*

~ LUKE 14:28

Lord Jesus, I know that You are not interested in good starters; it's the good finishers that You always look for. In John 19:30, You said, "It is finished," when you completed the greatest mission ever given. I don't know how close I am to the finish line of my life but I pray that I will finish strong in Your name and for Your glory.

— *Amen.* —

*Finishing well brings more glory to God than beginning well.*

# FEBRUARY
*Love Above All*

# LOVING OTHERS

*Anyone who does not love does not know God, for God is love.*

~ 1 JOHN 4:8 NLT

Heavenly Father, thank You from the bottom of my heart for loving me. In fact, You love me so much that You were even prepared to send Your blessed Son, Jesus, down from His home in heaven to rescue me from eternal hell and damnation. I really don't have enough words to thank You. By Your loving grace in me, I intend to love others as You have loved me.

*Amen.*

*Christian love, either towards God or towards man, is an affair of the will.*
– C. S. Lewis

# TRULY LOVING GOD

*"If you love Me, keep My commandments."*

~ JOHN 14:15

Lord Jesus, I do love You so
very much. Please forgive me
when I unintentionally break
Your commandments. Holy Spirit,
please help me to live a life that will
bring glory to Jesus, because I do love
Him with all my heart. Also, guide me
in obeying His Word in everything I do.

— *Amen.* —

*True love for Christ will mean hatred of sin.*
– John Benton

# NOT ASHAMED

*For I am not ashamed of this Good News about Christ. It is the power of God at work, saving everyone who believes – the Jew first and also the Gentile.*

~ ROMANS 1:16 NLT

Master, I love You so very much that
I desire to shout it from the rooftops.
Help me to share the Good News
with passion and conviction.
Please help me to never be ashamed
of the gospel, even in the face of
opposition and ridicule from others.

 *Amen.*

*If we love Christ, our devotion will
never remain a secret to this world.*

# SIMPLY ASK HIM

*"Call to Me, and I will answer you, and show you great and mighty things, which you do not know."*
~ JEREMIAH 33:3

Precious Jesus, so many times
we've had to go by faith, praying a
prayer of faith. Whether it was
for rain in drought-stricken areas,
salvation for family members
or strength to face what seems
like a mountain to us. And every
time our faith was rewarded;
You answered our call and provided
for us. What incredible love!

*Amen.*

*Beware in your prayers,
above everything else, of limiting God,
not only by unbelief, but by fancying
that you know what He can do.*
– Andrew Murray

# THE GREATEST LOVE STORY

*"For God so loved the world that He gave His only begotten Son, that whoever believes in Him should not perish but have everlasting life."*

~ JOHN 3:16

Father, I have no doubt whatsoever that this is the greatest story of pure love ever told. To think that You gave Your beloved Son, Jesus, to save a wretch like me from going to a lost eternity. It is something I find very hard to comprehend. But all I can say is thank You very much. I trust that I will not waste this priceless gift given for me.

— *Amen.* —

*Amazing Grace, Christ Jesus paid a debt that I could never pay.*
– Ellis J. Crum

# SAFE IN HIS LOVE

*There is no fear in love; but perfect love casts out fear.*

~ 1 JOHN 4:18

Dearest Lord Jesus, thank You for loving me so much! When I am in Your presence, I feel so safe and content. Fear has no place in my life when my eyes and my heart are focused on Your never-changing love for me. Help me to never forget the amazing love You have for me. I truly desire to spend more time in communion with You, my dear Friend.

— *Amen.* —

*The chains of love are stronger than the chains of fear.*
– William Gurnall

# LOVE YOUR HATERS

*If someone says, "I love God," but hates a fellow believer, that person is a liar.*

~ 1 JOHN 4:20 NLT

Father God, I pray today that You will help me to love my fellow man unconditionally, no matter what he has done to me, because that is exactly the way You love me. It is very easy to love those who love me but to love those who dislike me is a totally different story. I really do not want to be branded a liar. Please increase my love.

— *Amen.* —

*Love does not say, "Give me," but, "Let me give to you."*

# SHOW THEM LOVE

*"If I then, your Lord and Teacher, have washed your feet, you also ought to wash one another's feet."*

~ JOHN 13:14

Lord Jesus, You always lead by example. And by washing the dirty feet of Your creation, You are showing me that love is not just a word, but that true love is faith in action. It is not enough to tell people that I love them; I need to show them that I love them! Help me to do that today.

— *Amen.* —

*Many love at their tongue's end,*
*but the godly love at their finger's end.*

# FEED HIS LAMBS

*"Simon, son of Jonah, do you love Me more than these?" He said to Him, "Yes, Lord; You know that I love You." He said to him, "Feed My lambs."*

~ JOHN 21:15

Master, today You have challenged
me yet again, even as You
challenged Peter, the big fisherman
on the shore of the Sea of Tiberias
all those years ago, to feed Your
lambs and to do it unconditionally.
With Your help, Lord Jesus,
I shall do it till the day I die.

— *Amen.* —

*You can give without loving,
but you cannot love without giving.*
– Amy Carmichael

# PATIENCE AND KINDNESS

*Love is patient and kind. Love is not jealous or boastful or proud.*

~ 1 Corinthians 13:4 nlt

Father God, please help us to
be patient, especially in these
stressful times in which we are living.
Everybody wants everything
immediately and no one wants
to wait. Also, help us to be kind to our
fellow man, knowing that we are living
in evil times. It is a great opportunity
to shine for You, Lord, in a dark world.

— *Amen.* —

*Patience is not passive; on the contrary,
it is active; it is concentrated strength.*

# LOVE ABOVE ALL

*And now abide faith, hope, love, these three; but the greatest of these is love.*

~ 1 Corinthians 13:13

Father God, there is no doubt at all that the greatest power in all the world is pure love. Faith and hope are also so very important to get through the trials and tribulations of this life. But it is the undefiled love of Jesus Christ alone that shall see us through! Thank You for loving us unconditionally.

*Amen.*

*If we love Christ much,*
*surely we shall trust Him much.*
– Thomas Brooks

# A TEST OF LOVE

*Now it came to pass after these things that God tested Abraham.*

~ GENESIS 22:1

Father, even as You tested the love that Abraham had for You, that is how You can measure the depth of love a person has for You. Abraham was prepared to sacrifice his son, Isaac, whom he had patiently waited for, because of his undivided love for You. What amazing love! Please help us, Your people, to do the same.

*Amen.*

*The greatest and best thing that can be said of a person is that they loved the Lord.*

# A NEW LIFE

*Therefore, if anyone is in Christ, he is a new creation; old things have passed away; behold, all things have become new.*

~ 2 CORINTHIANS 5:17

Our dearest Lord Jesus, how we
love You so very much! The day
I gave my life to You was the day
I fell completely in love with You.
It is the very best decision that
any person can ever make. It has
changed me completely and forever.
Thank You, Master, I really do
know that I am a new creation.

—  —

*To adore God means we love Him
with all the powers within us.*
– A. W. Tozer

# A GREAT ACT OF LOVE

*Therefore the Lord Himself will give you a sign:*
*Behold, the virgin shall conceive and bear a Son,*
*and shall call His name Immanuel.*

~ ISAIAH 7:14

Father, this most incredible act of
love was prophesied hundreds
of years before Jesus was born.
How can man doubt the divinity
of Christ! Thank You, Father, for this
amazing gift. We really do appreciate
this greatest of all miracles.

*Amen.*

*The great of this world are those who*
*simply loved God more than others did.*
– A. W. Tozer

# THE FINEST DETAIL

*"But the very hairs of your head are all numbered. Do not fear therefore; you are of more value than many sparrows."*

~ LUKE 12:7

Father God, it is such a wonderful assurance to know that Jesus loves us so much that He knows and cares for the finest detail of our lives. Thank You, Lord, that You are the Author of all creation and yet still love us so much that You notice every detail of our lives.

*Amen.*

*No detail of your life is too insignificant for your heavenly Father's attention; no circumstance is so big that He cannot control it.*
– Jerry Bridges

# BEARING FRUIT

*But the fruit of the Spirit is love.*

~ GALATIANS 5:22

Father God, You have told us clearly
that we are to produce the fruit of
the Spirit. There are nine fruit, but the
first one is love. Thank You for showing
us true love by example – You gave us
Your only begotten Son. Please help
us to produce the fruit of love.

*Amen.*

*Have you ever noticed the difference
in the Christian life between work
and fruit? A machine can do work;
only a life can bear fruit.*
– Andrew Murray

# LOVING EVERYONE

*"Let the little children come to Me, and do not forbid them; for of such is the kingdom of heaven."*

~ MATTHEW 19:14

Lord Jesus, I just love the way You
entertain every person, whether child,
pensioner, stateman or pauper.
It does not matter to You where
they come from, You love all
people unconditionally.
Please help me to do the same.

 *Amen.*

*As soon as the love of God was shed
abroad in my soul, I loved all of
whatsoever denomination, who loved
the Lord Jesus in sincerity of heart.*
– George Whitefield

# RESTING IN HIM

*"Come to Me, all you who labor and are heavy laden, and I will give you rest."*

~ Matthew 11:28

Dear Lord Jesus, I remember the day I met You personally as my Savior like it was yesterday. I experienced love like I had never known before and I shall never, ever forget that moment. Thank You that from that day I found my rest in You and I have never walked alone.

— *Amen.*

*God, You have made us for Yourself,*
*and our hearts are restless till*
*they find their rest in You.*
– Saint Augustine

# AN INCREDIBLE LOVE

*In this is love, not that we loved God, but that He loved us and sent His Son to be the propitiation for our sins.*

~ 1 JOHN 4:10

Father God, there is one thing that I find so incredible to accept and that is that You, in fact, loved us first (see 1 John 4:19). When we were still sinners, You loved and cared for every part of our lives, to the extent that You sent Jesus to help us. Thank You very much, Father.

*Amen.*

*Saving us is the greatest and most concrete demonstration of God's love, the definitive display of His grace throughout time and eternity.*
– David Jeremiah

# LOVING MY NEIGHBOR

*"Love your neighbor as yourself. I am the Lord."*
~ Leviticus 19:18 NLT

Father God, this is not always an easy command to obey, simply because some of our neighbors are not easy folk to get on with. Sometimes it is a matter of trying to show love to those we don't really like. Please help me to love and to like my neighbor, Father.

*Amen.*

*He who does not love sinners cannot pray aright for them.*
– Charles Spurgeon

# THE GREATEST COMMANDMENT

*"You shall love the LORD your God with all your heart, with all your soul, and with all your strength."*

~ DEUTERONOMY 6:5

Dear Father God, without a doubt this is the greatest of all commandments in the Bible – there is nothing greater. It is such a great privilege to know You and to love You. The more I get to know You, Father, the more I am in love with You because You are such a good Father!

*Amen.*

*There is no better test of growth than that a man desires God because He is God.*
– D. Martyn Lloyd-Jones

# A JOYOUS LOVE

*Let all those rejoice who put their trust in You; let them ever shout for joy, because You defend them; let those also who love Your name be joyful in You.*
*~ Psalm 5:11*

Heavenly Father, it is such a joy to love You, because You are such a good and kind God. When I spend time with You in prayer, afterwards my heart is filled with unspeakable joy and gladness. The joy of the Lord is my strength (see Nehemiah 8:10).

*Amen.*

*Lord, take away from me all joy which does not come directly from the Lord Jesus.*
– Oswald Chambers

# THE IMPORTANCE OF WISDOM

*Don't turn your back on wisdom, for she will pro-tect you. Love her, and she will guard you.*

~ PROVERBS 4:6 NLT

Father God, You are speaking here
about wisdom. You are Wisdom,
so if we do not forsake You and the
wisdom from Your Word, but love
and respect You, then we shall
be protected in our daily lives.
To love You is wisdom.

*Amen.*

*No man is really wise unless he lives
in the will and for the glory of God.*
– Geoffrey Grogan

# A DECLARATION OF LOVE

*Jesus answered and said to him, "If anyone loves Me, he will keep My word; and My father will love him."*

~ JOHN 14:23

Lord Jesus, I love You and the
heavenly Father with all my heart.
I really love You so much,
my dearest Friend. In fact,
I could not even live one
day without You in my life.
You bring me so much peace,
love and purpose for living.

— *Amen.* —

*If we love Christ, our devotion
will not remain a secret.*

# IT WILL ALL WORK OUT

*We know that all things work together for good
to those who love God, to those who are the called
according to His purpose.*

~ Romans 8:28

Father, I have really experienced
this particular Scripture verse to
be so very accurate. The more I
love and respect You and Your
commandments, the better the things
of life seem to go for me. When I
face challenges, I know that You will
work things out and I don't need to
worry. It makes sense because You,
Father, are the absolute Creator.

 *Amen.*

*Faith is the root of all blessings.
Believe, and you shall be saved; believe,
and you must needs be satisfied.*
– Jeremy Taylor

# UNFAILING LOVE

*Can anything ever separate us from Christ's love?*
*~ Romans 8:35 nlt*

Our dearest Savior and Lord Jesus,
many have tried and not succeeded
in separating us from Your love.
Not persecution, not tribulation,
not famine and not even the
sword can separate us from You.
Because of Your unfailing love for us,
Your very own, we are more than
conquerors through You who loves
us so much (see Romans 8:37).

 — *Amen.* —

*Nothing can separate you from God's love,*
*absolutely nothing. God is enough for time,*
*God is enough for eternity. God is enough!*
– Hannah Whitall Smith

# BLESSING UPON BLESSING

*Eye has not seen, nor ear heard, nor have entered into the heart of man the things which God has prepared for those who love Him.*

~ 1 CORINTHIANS 2:9

Father, what a magnificent promise
You have given to Your followers.
I can give testimony to this
Scripture verse. You have already
blessed me right out of my socks.
When I first surrendered my life
to You, I had no idea of the
numerous blessings and wonderful
experiences You would give me.
Thank You again and again!

— *Amen.* —

*My carnal eye still cannot believe the miracles Jesus has done in my mortal life.*

# GRACE TO LOVE OTHERS

*"You shall love your neighbor as yourself."*
~ MATTHEW 19:19

Jesus, You have told us quite clearly
that we cannot honestly say we
love You whom we have not seen
and yet not love our neighbor
whom we have seen. Please give
us grace enough to love those
who do not love us, even if they
are our enemies. We do not desire
to disappoint You, Master.

*Amen.*

*We love everybody, because He first
loved us … And that is how the love of
God melts down the unlovely heart in
man, and begets in him the new creature.*
– Henry Drummond

# MARCH

*A Steadfast Faith*

# MORE FAITH

*But without faith it is impossible to please Him,*
*for he who comes to God must believe that He is,*
*and that He is a rewarder of those who diligently*
*seek Him.*

~ HEBREWS 11:6

Father God, if there is one
valuable lesson I have learned
since becoming one of Your followers,
it is that without faith in You and
in Your Holy Word, nothing works.
But on the other hand, if we believe
in You and Your Word, we can move
mountains (see Matthew 17:20).
Then nothing will be impossible
for us. More faith please, Lord.

*Amen.*

*Feed your faith and your*
*doubts will starve to death.*

# TRUSTING MORE

*For in it the righteousness of God is revealed from faith to faith; as it is written, "The just shall live by faith."*

~ ROMANS 1:17

Dear Jesus, I know that You do not just want our good works; You actually say that they are like filthy rags (see Isaiah 64:6). You want us, Your children, to trust You by faith alone. Faith is a lifestyle, it's not just a word. Please help us, Holy Spirit, to trust Jesus more.

—— *Amen.* ——

*One grain of faith is more precious than a pound of knowledge.*
– Joseph Hall

# SHARING GOD'S WORD

*So then faith comes by hearing, and hearing by the word of God.*

~ ROMANS 10:17

Father God, so many people want to know how they might gain faith. I know that the answer can be found in this above Scripture: Faith comes by hearing Your Holy Word. We need to read the Word daily and tell others the Good News that they may gain faith too. Please guide me in sharing Your Word with others.

*Amen.*

*We live by faith, and faith lives by exercise.*
– William Gurnall

# BUILDING UP FAITH

*Now faith is the substance of things hoped for, the*
*evidence of things not seen.*

~ HEBREWS 11:1

Dear Father, it is absolutely impossible
to believe the Bible without faith –
to believe a man can walk on water,
or that the Red Sea can be separated
with just a word, or that a young
maiden can be pregnant without
knowing a man. Please continue to
build up our faith in You, Father God.

*Amen.*

*Faith is to believe what you do not*
*yet see; the reward for this faith*
*is to see what you believe.*
– Saint Augustine

# TRUSTING GOD IN EVERYTHING

*So Jesus answered and said to them, "Have faith in God."*

~ MARK 11:22

Father God, I really want to share with You from the depths of my heart. I do not have any faith in anyone or anything else apart from You alone, my God and my Redeemer. In fact, I cannot even trust myself, and as the days are becoming more uncertain, I am trusting by faith in You alone, Father!

*Amen.*

*On Christ the Solid Rock I stand,
all other ground is sinking sand.*
– Edward Mote

# PATIENTLY WAIT

*He did not waver at the promise of God through unbelief, but was strengthened in faith, giving glory to God.*

~ ROMANS 4:20

Lord Jesus, no wonder Abraham was called the father of faith. He waited patiently for the promise of God that he would indeed receive a son and eventually, he did. Please help us to become more patient, because we lose out so many times in life because we just will not wait.

— *Amen.* —

*If we desire an increase of faith,
we must consent to its testings.*

# ALL GLORY TO GOD

*By faith Moses, when he became of age, refused to be called the son of Pharaoh's daughter.*

~ HEBREWS 11:24

Dear Father God, even reading of the great exploits of Moses, we see that he continually walked by faith and not by sight. That is why You persevered with him, Father. Everything we attempt for You, Lord, should be done by faith so that when it is seen, You get all the glory.

— *Amen.* —

*For a great miracle, the condition has to be impossibility – like splitting the Red Sea.*

# STAND ON GOD'S PROMISES

*By faith Noah, being divinely warned of things not yet seen, moved with godly fear.*

~ HEBREWS 11:7

Lord Jesus, we really need the kind of faith that Noah had in these very turbulent times in which we are living. People are so afraid and uncertain; they are being intimidated by the media, rumors and all kinds of theories. Like Noah of old, please help us to stand on Your promises alone, Lord.

— *Amen.* —

*Standing on the promises that cannot fail. When the howling storms of doubt and fear assail, by the living Word of God I shall prevail, standing on the promises of God.*
– Russell Carter

# CHOOSING TO TRUST

*By faith Enoch was taken away so that he did not see death, and was not found, because God had taken him.*

~ HEBREWS 11:5

O Father, because Enoch pleased You, he was taken home to heaven to be with You. We, too, so much desire to please You and to one day live with You in heaven. We know that You desire us to walk by faith and not by sight (see 2 Corinthians 5:7), as those who know You personally do. Holy Spirit, please fill us with more faith, we pray.

— *Amen.* —

*If our faith does not scare us,*
*then it is not big enough.*

# FAITH TO OBEY

*So He said, "Come." And when Peter had come down out of the boat, he walked on the water to go to Jesus.*

~ MATTHEW 14:29

Dear Lord Jesus, as You called Peter to walk on the water and he obeyed, we so much want to please and obey You too! Help us to have the enormous faith to obey You when You call us to do things that are quite impossible in human terms but quite normal in faith terms.

— *Amen.* —

*You must attempt something so big that if it's not from God, it's doomed to fail. Why? Because if it works, God gets all the glory.*

# TIME ON THE MOUNTAIN

*"The LORD will fight for you, and you shall hold your peace."*

~ EXODUS 14:14

O Lord Jesus Christ, what an incredible faith statement Moses made! This could only be said by someone who has spent much time with our Father on the mountain. Then the incredible miracle of faith happened, the sea parted and the Israelites walked through on dry ground. Fill us with Your presence as we, too, spend more time with God and trust Him to see us through every difficulty and moment of celebration.

*Amen.*

*First the mountain, then the ministry.*

# BLIND FAITH

*Then Jesus said to him, "Go your way; your faith has made you well." And immediately he received his sight and followed Jesus on the road.*

~ MARK 10:52

> Dear Father God, many of us today are as blind as Bartimaeus; we, too, need to have our blind eyes of faith opened so that we can follow Jesus. Please help us for we know we shall never succeed in this life of turmoil and fear without faith in You, Jesus.
>
> — *Amen.* —

*Faith is the identifying mark of the Christian.*
– Ronald Dunn

# FORTIFIED FAITH

*But Jesus turned around, and when he saw her he said, "Be of good cheer daughter; your faith has made you well."*

~ MATTHEW 9:22

Dear Father God, many times it is recorded in Your Holy Bible that Your Son, Jesus, said, "Your faith has made you well." Our prayer today is very simple: Please increase our faith to believe for the miracle we desperately need in our own lives.

 *Amen.*

*Faith is fostered by prayer, fortified by the study of the Word, and is fulfilled by our yielding, moment by moment, to the Lord Jesus Himself.*
– J. Charles Stern

# A KINGDOM CHILD

*Most men will proclaim each his own goodness,*
*but who can find a faithful man?*

~ PROVERBS 20:6

Dear Master, we pray that we
shall be found faithful by You,
not like men who proclaim their
own goodness, who speak of their
own achievements and accolades.
But that we would realize that without
Your intervention and divine grace,
we would fail every single time.

*Amen.*

*Faithfulness is our business;*
*fruitfulness is an issue that we must*
*be content to leave with God.*

– J. I. Packer

# FIGHT THE GOOD FIGHT

*I have fought the good fight, I have finished the race,
I have kept the faith.*

~ 2 TIMOTHY 4:7

My dearest Father God, our
greatest desire is to be able to say
with Your faithful servant Paul that
we, too, have fought the good
fight, completed our race and,
most importantly, kept the faith. We do
not want to disappoint You, Father!

— *Amen.* —

*God has no larger field for the man who is
not faithfully doing his work where he is.*

# I BELIEVE!

*Now he did not do many mighty works there because of their unbelief.*

~ MATTHEW 13:58

Dear Father, when I read in the Scriptures that Your beloved Son, Jesus, could perform very few mighty works in His own hometown because of the people's unbelief, I realize again how important it is to walk the faith walk, otherwise we will lose so badly. Thank You once again for sending us Your Helper, the Holy Spirit, who helps us walk in faith.

*Amen.*

*Since no man is excluded from calling upon God the gate of salvation is open to all. There is nothing else to hinder us from entering, but our own unbelief.*
– John Calvin

# FAITH IN ACTION

*But someone will say, "You have faith, and I have works." Show me your faith without your works, and I will show you my faith by my works.*

~ JAMES 2:18

Lord Jesus, it is so very true that faith without action is not really faith at all. Just like nothing will germinate apart from weeds unless we put the seed in the ground, so too faith without works is meaningless. Please help me to always follow up my faith with action. Yes, to have "faith like potatoes," practical faith.

*Amen.*

*An untried faith is a worthless faith.*
– Ron Dunn

# TAKING STOCK

*Examine yourself as to whether you are in the faith.*

~ 2 Corinthians 13:5

Lord Jesus, it is so easy to start off this faith walk, but quite a different story to finish this walk for God by simple faith. It is such a positive exercise to sit down and take stock of our lives at this present moment. Help us to examine our lives, taking the plank out of our own eyes before we attempt to take the speck out of our brother's eye (see Matthew 7:5).

*Amen.*

*The proof of real faith is a persistent mindset to obey what Jesus has taught us in His Word.*

# THE NAME OF JESUS

*"And His name, through faith in His name, has made this man strong."*

~ Acts 3:16

Dear Father God, there is so much power and faith in Your Son's name. Please forgive us for not using it more often when praying. There is no other name on earth or in heaven by which a man or woman might be saved. At the very name of Jesus, the dead are raised to life and sickness flees.

*Amen.*

*All God's giants have been weak men who did great things for God because they reckoned on God being with them.*
– James Hudson Taylor

# FAITH MATTERS

*For we say that faith was accounted to Abraham for righteousness.*

~ Romans 4:9

Father God, we have heard it said many times before that good men do not go to heaven, believers do. It does not matter who we are or what we do; what matters is whether we believe Jesus Christ to be the Son of God or not! And we truly do believe that Jesus is the Messiah and that He is coming again soon!

*Amen.*

*Until men have faith in Christ,
their best services are but glorious sins.*
– Thomas Brooks

# A GOOD WITNESS

*It shall be established forever like the moon, even like the faithful witness in the sky.*

~ Psalm 89:37

Dear Father God, through the power of Your Holy Spirit, please help me to be a better witness for Jesus Christ here on earth. Just like the moon is a beautiful reflection of the sun, so too do I want to be a beautiful reflection of Your Son, Jesus Christ, here on earth.

*Amen.*

*Get the queen bee of faith and all the other virtues will attend her.*

– Charles Spurgeon

# SACRED GIFTS FROM GOD

*For by grace you have been saved through faith,*
*and that not of yourselves; it is the gift of God, not*
*of works, lest anyone should boast.*

~ EPHESIANS 2:8-9

Heavenly Father, thank You for saving
sinners like us. For Your divine grace,
undeserved lovingkindness and
even our very faith is a wonderful
gift from You. Please, Holy Spirit,
do not ever allow me to take
these sacred gifts for granted.

— *Amen.* —

*Faith, having God with her,*
*is in a clear majority.*
– Charles Spurgeon

# GOD IS FAITHFUL

*Let us hold fast the confession of our hope without*
*wavering, for He who promised is faithful.*

~ HEBREWS 10:23

Dear Father God, You are just so very
faithful. Your steadfast faithfulness is an
area I esteem You greatly in. And that
is why I am more than happy to shout
it out from the very rooftops – my God
is faithful and true! Our mighty God
in whose name we say, Amen.

— *Amen.* —

*Of all the graces, faith honors*
*Christ most; therefore of all graces*
*Christ honors faith most.*
– Matthew Henry

# JESUS IS ALIVE

*Why do you seek the living among the dead? He is
not here, but He is risen!*

~ LUKE 24:5-6

Dear Lord Jesus, please forgive us
for so often looking for You among
the dead. You are not dead; in fact,
You are very much alive. Please help
us to become more like Paul, Your
faithful apostle, who boldly said, "For to
me, to live is Christ, and to die is gain."
As Your children, we do not fear death
but gladly welcome it as the bridge
between this life and eternity with You.

 *Amen.*

*Faith makes invisible things, visible;
absent things, present; things which are
afar off, to be very near unto the soul.*
– Thomas Brooks

# FAITH AS A MUSTARD SEED

*"If you have faith as a mustard seed, you can say to this mulberry tree, 'Be pulled up by the roots and be planted in the sea,' and it would obey you."*
~ LUKE 17:6

Lord Jesus, we all need little bottles of mustard seeds to share with people to encourage them to keep on trusting You by faith! But I myself so often seem to lack faith. Please help me to continue to practice what I preach, for Your glory alone. And I also know only too well that faith is not faith until it has been thoroughly tried and tested.

*Amen.*

*Faith is to prayer what the feather is to the arrow.*
– Thomas Watson

# IMMOVABLE FAITH

*Abraham never wavered in believing God's promise. In fact, his faith grew stronger, and in this he brought glory to God.*

~ ROMANS 4:20 NLT

Dear Father God, when Abraham
was put under severe pressure,
his faith held; it did not waver one
little bit. Please help us, Your children,
to do the same, to stand on Your
promises by faith, not doubting
one little bit. Even if the promise
takes some time to be fulfilled!

—— *Amen.* ——

*Oh, that unbelievers would learn
of faithful Abraham, and believe
whatever is revealed from God,
though they cannot fully comprehend it!*
– George Whitefield

# CALLING GOD

*"Call to Me and I will answer you, and show you
great and mighty things, which you do not know."*

~ JEREMIAH 33:3

Father God, indeed, we say that
Jeremiah 33:3 is Your heavenly
telephone number. We pray
earnestly that we will never ever stop
calling You for all kinds of requests.
We won't just call, but rather call by
simple faith, knowing full well that
You always listen. Thank You, Father!

— *Amen.* —

*God's phone line is never
too busy to take our calls.*

# THE MIRACLE WORKER

*For with God nothing will be impossible.*

*~ Luke 1:37*

Father, it is not possible to believe
in the truth of the Bible without pure
and undiluted faith. For example,
to believe the impossible, like a
young virgin girl falling pregnant
without knowing a man. In the eyes
of the world this is totally impossible,
but through the eyes of the
Miracle Worker, it is totally possible.

*Amen.*

*The true Christian should not seek
proofs for his faith, but rather be
firmly content with Scripture.*
– John Hus

# CLIMBING MOUNTAINS

*"But My servant Caleb, because he has a different spirit in him and has followed Me fully, I will bring into the land where he went, and his descendants shall inherit it."*

~ NUMBERS 14:24

Dear Father, we too desire to be Your people with a different spirit. When Caleb was given the privilege of choosing any part of the Promised Land to settle in, he asked for the big mountains, where the big giants lived. What great faith! Strengthen our faith in You so that we might do the same.

 *Amen.*

*Faith rests on the naked word of God. That word believed gives full assurance.*
– Harry Ironside

# WHAT GREAT FAITH!

*For who is this uncircumcised Philistine, that he should defy the armies of the living God?*

~ 1 SAMUEL 17:26

Dear Lord Jesus, thank You for the example of the faith of the young shepherd boy David. He had more faith than the entire Israelite army. It was because he was not focused on the giant, but rather on his God, Jehovah, the giant killer. May we also remain focused on You always no matter what we are facing.

— *Amen.* —

*We see giants, but the man of faith sees only mere grasshoppers!*

## STEP OUT IN FAITH

*"Ask, and it will be given to you; seek, and you will find; knock, and it will be opened to you."*

~ MATTHEW 7:7

---

Father God, one of the biggest hindrances to walk by faith is foolish pride. Too proud to ask, to seek or to knock, and the saddest thing is that You, Master, are standing by to assist us as soon as we step out in faith. Please help our unbelief!

 *Amen.*

---

*Faith is not anti-intellectual.*
*It is an act of man that reaches*
*beyond the limits of our five senses.*
– Billy Graham

# APRIL

*Patience to Endure*

# CULTIVATING PATIENCE

*We can rejoice, too, when we run into problems and trials, for we know that they help us develop endurance.*

~ ROMANS 5:3 NLT

Lord Jesus, even as Paul,
Your special apostle, said that he
rejoiced in hardships and trials
because it produced patient
endurance in his life, I too thank
You for it is truly only through the
hardships in our lives that we learn
how to become patient people.

*Amen.*

*Patience is the companion of wisdom.*
– Saint Augustine

# PATIENTLY WAITING

*"Having heard the word with a noble and good heart, keep it and bear fruit with patience."*

~ LUKE 8:15

Dear Father God, I understand the principle of patience very clearly. Like the farmer, we will never reap a good and fruitful crop of any kind if we do not have patience. We have to wait until the fruit is ripe and mature, otherwise we will damage it and risk losing it altogether.

— *Amen.* —

*Patience is a virtue that carries a lot of "wait".*

# THE FRUIT OF PATIENCE

*Then you will not become spiritually dull and indifferent. Instead, you will follow the example of those who are going to inherit God's promises because of their faith and endurance.*

~ HEBREWS 6:12 NLT

Heavenly Father, I realize that we, like the saints before us, need to exercise patience, perseverance and faith if we are to receive our inheritance one day. It's not easy, Lord Jesus, but by the power of Your Holy Spirit, I believe that we can achieve it. Hallelujah!

*Amen.*

*Our patience will achieve more than our force.*
– Edmund Burke

# WHAT WE STAND FOR

*For examples of patience in suffering, dear brothers and sisters, look at the prophets who spoke in the name of the Lord.*

~ JAMES 5:10 NLT

Father God, we earnestly pray that
when the pressure is on to stand
up for Jesus and be counted, we
shall not be found wanting! But with
much patience and courage,
we might stand for truth and for
righteousness in the love of Christ.

———— *Amen*. ————

*Teach us, O Lord, the disciplines of patience,
for to wait is often harder than to work.*
– Peter Marshall

# GOD'S COMMANDMENTS

*Here is the patience of the saints; here are those who keep the commandments of God and the faith of Jesus.*

~ REVELATION 14:12

Heavenly Father, we desire so much to keep all of Your commandments in these last days, no matter how hard it will become. Please increase our faith to stand strong and our patience to undertake whatever persecution will come to us in these last days.

— *Amen.* —

*Our impatience only learns patience through the thorn of delay and darkness.*
– J. Charles Stern

# GROWING THROUGH TRIALS

*Count it all joy when you fall into various trials,*
*knowing that the testing of your faith produces pa-*
*tience. But let patience have its perfect work, that*
*you may be perfect and complete, lacking nothing.*
~ JAMES 1:2-4

Dear Father, when we find ourselves
falling into all kinds of temptations
and trials, we pray earnestly that
we will undertake them with patient
endurance and not drop the ball,
so to speak. We pray that we will
grow through these times of difficulty
and that people will see us as patient
and enduring children of God.

— *Amen.* —

*Cheerful patience is a holy art*
*and skill, which man learns from God.*
– Thomas Manton

# HOPE IN THE SCRIPTURES

*Whatever things were written before were written for our learning, that we through the patience and comfort of the Scriptures might have hope.*

~ ROMANS 15:4

Father, we want to say a huge thank You for Your Holy Word, the Bible. The Scriptures really do bring immense patience, comfort and hope to our very inner being. When we feel stressed and uptight, reading Your Word makes us more patient and relaxed.

*Amen.*

*Hope is the mother of patience.*
– William Jenkyn

# PATIENCE PAYS OFF

*When Job prayed for his friends, the L*ORD *restored his fortunes. In fact, the L*ORD *gave him twice as much as before!*

~ JOB 42:10 NLT

Dear Master, I really do respect and look up to Your servant Job. When I think about what he went through and the incredible patience he displayed, it really challenges me to up my game, as the saying goes. You rewarded him so well for the patience displayed. Help me to show the same patience as he did.

— *Amen.* —

*Patience is the fruit and evidence of faith.*
– John Calvin

# LONG-DISTANCE RUNNERS

*Let us run with endurance the race God has set
before us.*

~ HEBREWS 12:1 NLT

Lord Jesus, the long-distance
runner understands about pacing
himself and, as a result, has to be
extremely patient because if he
is not, he will simply fail to reach
the finish line. Help us to take our
time so that we, too, will patiently
endure to the end, Master!

*Amen.*

*To lengthen my patience is the
best way to shorten my troubles.*
– George Swinnock

# THE WAITING GAME

*So let's not get tired of doing what is good. At just the right time we will reap a harvest of blessing if we don't give up.*

~ GALATIANS 6:9 NLT

Dear Lord Jesus, once again it is all about the waiting game, which requires disciplined patience in order to see the project completed successfully. Please help us not to rush at anything, but to remain steadfast and immovable.

*Amen.*

*Life is a symphony and we lose a third of it by cutting out the slow movement.*

# RENEWING OUR STRENGTH

*But those who wait on the LORD shall renew their strength.*

~ ISAIAH 40:31

Dear Lord Jesus, You are our absolute
example of one who is patient.
Constantly, You told Your disciples
to come aside and rest, to be quiet,
to patiently regroup as it were.
Because You knew they would not
make it if they impulsively carried on.
Please help us to patiently wait on You
and by so doing, renew our strength.

*Amen.*

*The times we find ourselves having to wait
on others may be the perfect opportunities
to train ourselves to wait on the Lord.*
– Joni Eareckson Tada

# WORTH WAITING FOR

*Be patient, brethren, until the coming of the Lord.*
*See how the farmer waits for the precious fruit of*
*the earth, waiting patiently for it until it receives*
*the early and latter rain.*

~ JAMES 5:7

Lord Jesus, thank You for reminding
me that so often we write off a
crop or a relationship or a vision
without giving it enough time to
come to full fruition. Like the patient
farmer, Lord, teach us to wait more
and not become so impulsive.

 *Amen.*

*The best crop is always worth waiting for*
*because it often takes the longest to ripen!*

# MORE THOUGHTFUL

*The end of a thing is better than its beginning; the patient in spirit is better than the proud in spirit.*

~ ECCLESIASTES 7:8

Dear Father God, we have seen it far too often – the proud are like "a bull in a china shop". But the patient in spirit tend to take their time and weigh things up before making a decision. Please, Holy Spirit, help us to become more thoughtful and patient, taking our time to weigh things up and to hear from the Father before we do anything.

*Amen.*

*It's the old adage of the tortoise and the hare – the patient and steady always finish first.*

# TEMPER, TEMPER!

*Better to be patient than powerful; better to have self-control than to conquer a city.*

*~ PROVERBS 16:32*

Dear Father God, please help us, Your children, to cultivate self-control and patience. As the Bible verse says, it's much better to control one's emotions than to take over control of an empire, having all the power in the world.

— *Amen.* —

*There are few things more distasteful in life than to see an arrogant person who has no regard for anyone else.*

# TRUST GOD'S TIMING

*Rest in the L*ORD*, and wait patiently for Him; do not fret because of him who prospers in his way.*

~ PSALM 37:7

Heavenly Father, please help us
to remain fixed on You alone, not
becoming anxious or stressed by those
who appear to prosper because
of their pushy and forward ways.
We know that if we patiently wait on
You alone, You will see us through.

———— *Amen.* ————

*The world's system of push
and pull never, ever succeeds!*

# PUT OTHERS FIRST

*Always be humble and gentle. Be patient with each other, making allowance for each other's faults because of your love.*

~ EPHESIANS 4:2 NLT

---

Dear Father, please help us to be patient and full of love towards one another, not being selfish or self-centered and putting our own agendas before that of others'. Help us to rather prefer others to ourselves, making allowance for their faults and loving them as You love us.

*Amen.*

---

*Your Word is very clear, that the last shall be first, and the first shall be last (see Matthew 20:16)!*

# DON'T GIVE UP!

*Add to your faith virtue, to virtue knowledge, to knowledge self-control, to self-control perseverance, to perseverance godliness.*

~ 2 Peter 1:5-6

Dear Father, please help us to become a disciplined people for Your glory. We have to focus on the work You have called us to. We must finish the job and no matter how long that might take, we are not to become impatient or to give up. No matter how long, we will overcome for Your glory alone.

— *Amen.* —

*Patient waiting is often the highest way of doing God's will.*
– Jeremy Collier

# FINISHING STRONG

*But I discipline my body and bring it into subjection, lest, when I have preached to others, I myself should become disqualified.*

~ 1 CORINTHIANS 9:27

Heavenly Father, like any
faithful athlete, we patiently desire
to finish this race without dropping
the baton. This is only possible if we
become steadfast. Please help us,
Master, to remain disciplined
so that we can finish strong.

*Amen.*

*Biblical patience is not rooted in
fatalism that says everything is out
of control. It is rooted in faith that
says everything is in God's control.*
– John Blanchard

# YOU ALWAYS HEAR ME

*I waited patiently for the Lord; and He inclined to me, and heard my cry.*

~ Psalm 40:1

Lord Jesus, one of the many reasons why we love You so very much is because You always hear our cry! You do not always answer us right away, but we wait patiently, because not once have You ignored our plea. Faithful God, how we love You.

*Amen.*

*Patience is not passive: on the contrary it is active; it is concentrated strength!*
– Edward G. Bulwer-Lytton

# HEAR ME OUT

*Paul started his defense: "I am fortunate, King Agrippa, that you are the one hearing my defense ... for I know you are an expert on all Jewish customs and controversies. Now please listen to me patiently!"*

~ ACTS 26:1-3 NLT

Dear Father, even as Paul was happy to give an account for himself, not needing any professional assistance, we also believe that You will give us the words of life and truth to speak out boldly to this dying world as we wait patiently for Your intervention.

*Amen.*

*Before one can display a quiet mouth he must first possess a quiet spirit, for out of the abundance of the spirit does the mouth speak.*
– Watchman Nee

# PATIENT SERVANTS

*He will judge everyone according to what they have done. He will give eternal life to those who keep on doing good, seeking after the glory and honor and immortality that God offers.*

~ ROMANS 2:6-7 NLT

Dear heavenly Father, please help us to be consistent in serving You patiently. You are looking for folk who are not fair-weather believers, but rather those who serve and love others to Your glory, especially those who cannot repay us for our kindness.

— *Amen.* —

*A Christian without patience is like a soldier without arms.*
– Thomas Watson

# GODLY ENDURANCE

*Now may the Lord direct your hearts into the love*
*of God and into the patience of Christ.*

~ 2 THESSALONIANS 3:5

Dear Lord Jesus, it is the patient
endurance of Your beautiful heart
that we all need at this critical hour.
For we are all only too aware that
it is only You in our hearts that
shall enable us to finish this earthly
journey successfully. More godly
endurance please, Master.

*Amen.*

*"Be still, and know that I am God."*
– Psalm 46:10

# A GENTLE HEART

*A servant of the Lord must not quarrel but must be kind to everyone, be able to teach, and be patient with difficult people.*

~ 2 TIMOTHY 2:24 NLT

Dearest Holy Spirit, our beloved Jesus desires us, His children, to not be quarrelsome, but to be gentle and to be an example to this dying world of what a child of God is supposed to look like. Please help us to become more patient and loving, we pray.

 *Amen.*

*We face the aggressive world with an opposite spirit, so that they may see that we have indeed been with Jesus Christ.*

# PATIENCE REWARDED

*Then Abraham waited patiently, and he received
what God had promised.*

~ HEBREWS 6:15 NLT

Dear Father, what an incredible
example of patience! Abraham
waited patiently for a son and heir.
God, You looked upon Your servant
with such love and satisfaction
that You rewarded him with Isaac,
and he became the father of
many nations. Help us to also
be patient as we wait for Your
promises in our lives to come true.

*Amen.*

*A handful of patience is worth
more than a bushel of brains.*
– Dutch proverb

# HARD WORKERS

*"And you have persevered and have patience, and have labored for My name's sake and have not become weary."*

~ REVELATION 2:3

Heavenly Father, there is no exception for hard work done in an excellent and patient manner. You have told us very clearly that You do not look favorably on lazy people. We, as Your children, desire to be found working very hard when You call us to go home.

*Amen.*

*"Work is a blessing. God has so arranged the world that work is necessary, and He gives us hands and strength to do it."*
– Elisabeth Elliot

# PATIENCE OF THE SAINTS

*Here is the patience of the saints; here are those who keep the commandments of God and the faith of Jesus.*

~ REVELATION 14:12

Our heavenly Father, this is the type of Christian You are looking for in these last days. Men and women who, much like the saints of old, keep all of Your commandments patiently as the great day of judgment grows ever closer. Please help us to have the patience of the saints.

— *Amen.* —

*All true servants of Christ must be content to wait for their wages.*
– J. C. Ryle

# FAITH TO PERFORM WONDERS

*Truly, the signs of an apostle were accomplished among you with all perseverance, in signs and wonders and mighty deeds.*

~ 2 Corinthians 12:12

Lord Jesus, when You walked
upon this earth, You were never
in a rush. You moved patiently
and performed many mighty and
miraculous signs and wonders.
Please increase our faith to do likewise
for Your wonderful name, Jesus.

*Amen.*

*Quietly and patiently, just like Jesus,
we desire to get on with the work
the Father has called us to do.*

# WITHOUT PROTEST

*He was led as a lamb to the slaughter, and as a sheep before its shearers is silent.*

~ Isaiah 53:7

O Master, what an example You are to us! You never tried to argue or to defend Yourself, You simply went to the cross with no fear or anxious sentiment and patiently died for our sins. What love and commitment! Please Lord, help us to do the same, to deny ourselves and follow You.

 *Amen.*

*We ought to give thanks for all fortune: if it is good, because it is good, if bad, because it works in us patience, humility and the contempt of this world.*
– C. S. Lewis

# DON'T LET GOD DOWN

*We also pray that you will be strengthened with all his glorious power so you will have all the endurance and patience you need. May you be filled with joy.*

~ Colossians 1:11 NLT

Dear Father, You have qualified us to be partakers and to have the inheritance with the saints! Lord, what an honor, but we are also well aware that with this privilege comes longsuffering and our prayer is that we do not let You down.

— *Amen.* —

*Patience is a grace as difficult as it is necessary, and as hard to come by as it is precious when it is gained.*

– Charles Spurgeon

# WATCHFUL SOLDIERS

*Pray in the Spirit at all times and on every occasion. Stay alert and be persistent in your prayers for all believers everywhere.*

~ EPHESIANS 6:18 NLT

Lord Jesus, there is no doubt whatsoever that we are in the fight of our lives. This is not a mere skirmish, but rather an ongoing war we are involved in. We are going to have to take our time, to be patient and to fight clever. Yes, we are overcomers, but at the same time we cannot take the enemy for granted. We walk patiently with You, Master.

*Amen.*

*We, as good soldiers of the cross, never take our eyes off the enemy.*

# MAY

*The Gift of Salvation*

# A NEW CREATION

*Therefore, if anyone is in Christ, he is a new creation; old things have passed away; behold, all things have become new.*

~ 2 Corinthians 5:17

Dear Father God, indeed, what an incredible miracle "new birth" is. I remember the day I was born again like it was yesterday. And it is just exactly how I feel – all new, clean, fresh and light of heart. Please help us to never slip or fall back into our old ways ever again.

*Amen.*

*It is not your hold of Christ that saves you, but His hold of you!*
– Charles Spurgeon

# AN INCREDIBLE GIFT

*"For God so loved the world that He gave His only begotten Son, that whoever believes in Him should not perish but have everlasting life."*

~ JOHN 3:16

Father, what an incredible gift –
the greatest gift that this desperate
world has ever received! "Thank You"
seems so inadequate, but we don't
actually have any other words.
Nothing less than a lifeline to the lost
and perishing, we thank You, Father.

*Amen.*

*Salvation originates not in man but in God.*
– Simon J. Kistemaker

# JESUS IS LORD

*If you confess with your mouth the Lord Jesus and believe in your heart that God raised Him from the dead, you will be saved.*

~ ROMANS 10:9

> Dearest Lord Jesus, we really do believe and are so proud to tell the whole world that You are no longer in the grave. You are risen and You are returning very soon for Your believing people who are not ashamed to speak up! Help us to use the opportunities You give us to confess that You are Lord.
>
> — *Amen.* —

*God saved us to make us holy, not happy.*
– Vance Havner

# THE GIFT OF GOD

*For by grace you have been saved through faith, and that not of yourselves; it is the gift of God, not of works, lest anyone should boast.*

~ EPHESIANS 2:8-9

Lord Jesus, what a wonderfully reassuring message! This Scripture verse is a good reminder that salvation is all about Your kindness to Your people and absolutely nothing of ourselves. Even the very faith we have was given to us by You. Thank You, Lord.

*Amen.*

*We are not saved by merit but by mercy.*
– John Blanchard

# FAITH IN ACTION

*Jesus responded, "Salvation has come to this home today, for this man has shown himself to be a true son of Abraham."*

~ LUKE 19:9 NLT

Dear Lord Jesus, Zacchaeus
showed You by his actions that
he had become one of Your
chosen sons. Not only by lip service,
but by action too. He actually
put his money (fourfold),
where his newfound faith was.
Please help us to do likewise.

 *Amen.*

*Faith in action is love, and love in action is service. By transforming that faith into living acts of love, we put ourselves in contact with God Himself, with Jesus our Lord.*
– Mother Teresa

# AMAZING SALVATION

*"And what do you benefit if you gain the whole world but lose your own soul?"*

~ MARK 8:36 NLT

Father God, we do not want to be found barking up the wrong tree when You come again in all Your glory. We want to be telling others about the amazing salvation found in Christ Jesus and not in the things of this dying world.

— *Amen.* —

*If salvation could be attained only by working hard, then surely horses and donkeys would be in heaven.*
– Martin Luther

# GOD FIGHTS FOR US

*And Moses said to the people, "Do not be afraid. Stand still, and see the salvation of the LORD, which He will accomplish for you today."*

~ Exodus 14:13

Father, it is such a wonderful thing to know that You are not only in our corner, but that You are also fighting for us, even as You did for the Israelites at the Red Sea. You are indeed such a loving and protective Father. Thank You that we don't need to be afraid.

*Amen.*

*The greatest of all miracles is the salvation of a soul.*
– Charles Spurgeon

# THE MEANING OF LIFE

*I long for Your salvation, O LORD, and Your law is my delight.*

~ PSALM 119:174

Dear heavenly Father, thank You
so very much for saving a wretch
like me. Where would any of us
be if it were not for our Savior,
Jesus, who gave His life for us.
We searched everywhere to find the
true meaning of this life and then
we found it in the Lord Jesus Christ.
Thank You for Your salvation, Lord.

*Amen.*

*Since no man is excluded from calling
upon God, the gate of salvation is open
to all. There is nothing else to hinder us
from entering, but our own unbelief.*
– John Calvin

# A HEART FOR THE UNSAVED

For *"whoever calls on the name of the* LORD *shall be saved."*

~ ROMANS 10:13

Father God, You have such a burden
for lost souls. You do not want one
single human being to be lost.
What a heart You have for Your very
own creation. We pray that You will
put that same love in our hearts for our
unsaved family members and friends.

———— *Amen.* ————

*Salvation is not deliverance from*
*hell alone, it is deliverance from sin.*
— Charles Spurgeon

# BETTER THINGS

*Beloved, we are confident that you are meant for
better things, things that come with salvation.*

~ HEBREWS 6:9

Father God, we know that You
expect much better things from us,
Your children. Please do not allow
us to disappoint You in what You
have given us to do, we pray.
For only the very best is good enough
for You, because You gave us the
very best, namely Jesus Christ.

*Amen.*

*God does not owe you salvation.
You deserve damnation,
but He provides salvation.*
– Billy Sunday

# GOD GIVES ETERNAL LIFE

*The Lord is my strength and song, and He has become my salvation.*

~ Exodus 15:2

Father, when we think of the way You have saved us through Jesus, Your Son, all we desire is to sing Your praise and worship You. Wherever we may be – in the factory, in the mine, in the field – we want to shout it out to the world that we have been given eternal life.

*Amen.*

*There are two hopeless things, salvation without Christ and salvation without holiness.*
– Charles Studd

# IN TIMES OF TROUBLE

*Our salvation also in the time of trouble.*

~ ISAIAH 33:2

Father God, I don't know how
many times You have been our
lifesaver in times of severe trouble
and intense hardship. And every
single day, not once have You
abandoned us or left us alone. In fact,
Master, it is the absolute opposite.
The more intense the fight, the more
Your love and salvation have kept us.

 *Amen.*

*Nowhere does the Bible tell us that*
*salvation is by a faith that does not work.*
– R. B. Kuiper

# THROUGH FAITH IN JESUS

*… Who are kept by the power of God through faith*
*for salvation ready to be revealed in the last time.*

~ 1 PETER 1:5

Father, thank You for reminding us
that it is through faith in Jesus alone
that we receive salvation, which we
will see in these last days in which
we are living. Please, Holy Spirit,
increase our faith to believe!

*Amen.*

*Though the Bible was written over*
*sixteen centuries by at least forty*
*authors, it has one central theme –*
*salvation through faith in Christ.*
– Max Lucado

# SALVATION FROM GOD

*Salvation belongs to the LORD.*

~ PSALM 3:8

Heavenly Father, yet once again
we realize that our salvation
can only come from one place.
That place is from heaven alone
for truly, salvation can be found
in no other place. Therefore, Lord,
please have Your way in our lives.

— *Amen.* —

*If there be ground for you to trust in your
own righteousness, then, all that Christ
did to purchase salvation, and all that God
did to prepare the way for it is in vain.*
– Jonathan Edwards

# DESPERATE FOR SALVATION

*I have waited for Your salvation, O LORD!*
~ GENESIS 49:18

Dear Lord Jesus, we have waited
for Your salvation for all our lives.
Many of us, when we were still far
away from You, not even aware
that we needed to be saved,
were so desperate. Thank You,
Master, for persisting with us,
never giving up on Your children.

*Amen.*

*The salvation of a single soul is
more important than the production
or preservation of all the epics
and tragedies in the world.*
– C. S. Lewis

# ARMOR OF GOD

*Put on salvation as your helmet, and take the swordof the Spirit, which is the word of God.*

~ EPHESIANS 6:17 NLT

Dear Lord Jesus, thank You for the armor You have given us to put on each new day. We are clearly reminded that we are in a full-scale war and need to put on the whole armor of God each morning before we leave home. Please help us to stand strong.

*Amen.*

*Salvation is a helmet not a nightcap.*
– Vance Havner

# CONFESSION OF FAITH

*For it is by believing in your heart that you are made right with God, and it is by openly declaring your faith that you are saved.*

~ ROMANS 10:10 NLT

Sweet Jesus, what a special privilege to be able to make, with our mouths, the audible confession of our faith. To hear voices confess their faith in You is the sweetest sound there is. Hallelujah!

 *Amen.*

*Believing and confessing go together; and you cannot be saved without you take them both. "With the mouth confession is made unto salvation."*
– Dwight Moody

# MESSAGE OF SALVATION

*Family of Abraham, and those among you who fear God, to you the word of this salvation has been sent.*

~ Acts 13:26

Almighty God, through Your precious Son, Jesus, You have made it possible that whosoever bows the knee and acknowledges You as Lord shall be saved. What an incredible door You have opened, a door for all men and women to receive salvation.

 *Amen.*

*Jesus is not one of many ways to approach God, nor is He the best of several ways; He is the only way.*
– A. W. Tozer

# SEEK THE LORD

*For my eyes have seen Your salvation which You have prepared before the face of all peoples, a light to bring revelation to the Gentiles, and the glory of Your people Israel.*

~ LUKE 2:30-32

Dear Lord Jesus, we so long to see what Your servant Simeon saw when he looked into Your beautiful face and saw the salvation of all mankind looking back at him. Come, Master, come. We are ready and waiting.

*Amen.*

*They never sought in vain
that sought the Lord alright!*
– Robert Burns

# CLOTHED IN GRACE

*I will greatly rejoice in the L*ORD*, my soul shall be joyful in my God; for He has clothed me with the garments of salvation.*

~ ISAIAH 61:10

Our dearest heavenly Father,
You have clothed us in garments
of salvation. You have taken away
our filthy rags of condemnation
and replaced them with clean,
uncontaminated clothes. You have
made us new and clean again.
Thank You, Father God!

 *Amen.*

*The Lord took our place that we
might have His peace; He took our sin
that we might have His salvation.*

# WELLS OF SALVATION

*Therefore with joy you will draw water from the wells of salvation.*

~ Isaiah 12:3

Master, what a beautiful reminder this Scripture is of Your encounter with the woman at the well. You told her that if she drank from the water You were offering her, that she would never thirst again. It is pure and unpolluted water and since we have been drinking from it, we've never been thirsty again.

*Amen.*

*Christ rose again, but our sins did not: they are buried forever in His grave.*
– John Brown

# GENUINE REPENTANCE

*For godly sorrow produces repentance leading to salvation, not to be regretted; but the sorrow of the world produces death.*

~ 2 CORINTHIANS 7:10

Sweet Jesus, we know only too well
that if there is no genuine repentance,
then there can be no forgiveness and
that means salvation is not possible.
Help us to never be too proud
or arrogant to say sorry, Lord.

— *Amen.* —

*The death of Jesus was not a proposition
for sinners but the purchase of salvation.*
– John Blanchard

# THE PINNACLE OF PEACE

*Now godliness with contentment is great gain.*
~ 1 Timothy 6:6

Father, probably the absolute pinnacle of peace and contentment in our lives came about on the memorable day when we received Your salvation in our lives. How could we possibly forget? Thank You to Jesus Christ, who made it a reality.

*Amen.*

*Christ is the desire of nations, the joy of angels, the delight of the Father. What solace then must that soul be filled with, that has the possession of Him to all eternity!*
– John Bunyan

# ROCK OF SALVATION

*He alone is my rock and my salvation, my fortress*
*where I will not be shaken.*

~ PSALM 62:6 NLT

Father God, living in these turbulent
times is not easy. Thank You very
much for being there for us.
You are our defense so we shall
not be moved or shaken. We will
not be moved, because if You
are for us, then who could stand
against us (see Romans 8:31)?

*Amen.*

*Security is not the absence of danger but the*
*presence of God, no matter what the danger.*

## HUMBLE IN SPIRIT

*For the LORD takes pleasure in His people; He will beautify the humble with salvation.*

~ PSALM 149:4

> Lord Jesus, we know that You resist the proud and the arrogant, but always give grace and salvation to the humble in spirit (see 1 Peter 5:5). In fact, You love and take great pleasure in humble, gentle folk and You make us beautiful in Your time.

*Amen.*

*The source of humility is the habit of realizing the presence of God.*
– William Temple

# THE TRUTH OF SALVATION

*In Him you also trusted, after you heard the word
of truth, the gospel of your salvation …*

~ EPHESIANS 1:13

Dear heavenly Father, after hearing
the wonderful news of salvation
to be found in Christ Jesus alone,
how could we do anything else save
that we would trust in You alone?
It is the simple truth of salvation
that has taken us out of the depths
of despair. We have hope in
Jesus alone. Thank You, Father.

— *Amen.* —

*Our salvation consists
in the doctrine of the Cross.*
– John Calvin

# WALK IN HOLINESS

*God from the beginning chose you for salvation through sanctification by the Spirit and belief in the truth.*

~ 2 THESSALONIANS 2:13

Father God, You have indeed
chosen us from the very beginning.
Thank You, Lord! You have
also called us to walk in holiness
(see 1 Peter 1:15-16), which is
the end product of obedience,
and this is our absolute intention:
To become holy men and women,
serving You with all our hearts.

 *Amen.*

*We must be holy, because this is the only sound evidence that we have a saving faith in our Lord Jesus Christ.*
– J. C. Ryle

# BEHOLD GOD'S BEAUTY

*And then all people will see the salvation sent from God.*

~ Luke 3:6 nlt

Lord Jesus, we cannot wait to see You in person. What an incredible day that will be! To think what You have done for us, we too, much like Your son King David, want to dwell in Your house, O Lord, and behold Your beauty all the days of our lives (see Psalm 27:4).

— *Amen.* —

*Christ died for men precisely because men are not worth dying for; to make them worth it.*
– C. S. Lewis

# THE DAY OF SALVATION

*Behold, now is the accepted time; behold, now is the day of salvation.*

~ 2 CORINTHIANS 6:2

Father God, we hear You loud and clear today: There is no time to waste. To say "tomorrow" is a very foolish way to think. For life is but a vapor – it is here today and gone tomorrow, just like the flowers in the field (see James 4:14). Help us, Master, to redeem the time. We have many folk to still speak to about the salvation of the Lord.

*Amen.*

*Oh, how precious is time, and how it pains me to see it slide away, while I do so little to any good purpose.*
– David Brainerd

# FAIR-WEATHER CHRISTIANS

*I will rejoice in the LORD! I will be joyful in the God of my salvation!*

~ HABAKKUK 3:18 NLT

Father, we belong to You unconditionally. We are not fair-weather Christians who will only serve You when everything is going well. We will praise and worship You no matter what. You are a good God and always work things out for our best in the end.

*Amen.*

*Jesus came not only to teach but to save, not only to reveal God to mankind, but also to redeem mankind for God.*

– John Stott

# ROCK OF OUR SALVATION

*Then they abandoned the God who had made them;*
*they made light of the Rock of their salvation.*

~ DEUTERONOMY 32:15 NLT

Sweet Jesus, far be it from us to
scorn the gift of eternal life through
our precious salvation, which You
have offered to us freely. What a
gross insult that would be, because
without salvation we are lost forever!
Thank You, Lord Jesus, for being
the Rock of our salvation, giving us
access to eternal life in heaven.

— *Amen.* —

*It is God alone who saves, and that in*
*every element of the saving process.*
– Benjamin B. Warfield

# JUNE
*The Power of Prayer*

# TEACH US TO PRAY

*"In this manner, therefore, pray: Our Father in heaven, hallowed be Your name …"*

~ MATTHEW 6:9

Lord Jesus, thank You for teaching us how to pray to our heavenly Father. Such a very beautiful and yet simple prayer, we pray it so very often. Thank You also for always leading us, Your children, by example and for teaching us to walk in Your footsteps.

*Amen.*

*Too often we forget to thank God for answered prayer. Praise is the proper punctuation mark for answered prayer.*
– Charles Spurgeon

# FERVENT PRAYER

*The effective, fervent prayer of a righteous man avails much.*

~ JAMES 5:16

Father God, You respond to earnest prayer; the kind of persistent, effective prayer that believes by faith that our prayer is going to be answered. Please increase our faith to pray more sincerely and fervently. The kind of prayer that, like Elijah's, can impact and change even the weather.

*Amen.*

*The prayer that begins with trustfulness, and passes on into waiting, will always end in thankfulness, triumph, and praise.*
– Alexander Maclaren

# GOING ASIDE TO PRAY

*I look up to the mountains – does my help come from there? My help comes from the LORD, who made heaven and earth!*

~ PSALM 121:1-2 NLT

Father God, we will not seek our help from the mountains, but rather directly from You alone. And it will come from direct prayer, Master. Thank You that You are always just one prayer away from us. No matter where we are, we can pray to You and You will hear us.

*Amen.*

*Faith in a prayer-hearing God will make a prayer-loving Christian.*
– Andrew Murray

# PRAY ALWAYS

*Pray without ceasing.*

~ 1 THESSALONIANS 5:17

Father God, thank You today for reminding us that the prayer life is actually a way of life. We don't just pray at a fixed time, like in the early morning or before we go to sleep in the evening. No, not at all; we pray while we plow the fields, milk the cows, study, do housework, serve in a shop … and especially when we sit and have a cup of tea or coffee.

— *Amen.* —

*Fervent prayers produce phenomenal results.*
– Woodrow Kroll

# CALLING GOD

*"Call to Me, and I will answer you, and show you*
*great and mighty things, which you do not know."*
~ JEREMIAH 33:3

Dear Father, it is wonderful to know
that You invite us to call on You.
You are available to listen to us all
the time. You are never too busy to
hear us. If we pray to You at any time,
night or day, You always take our calls.
That's why we love You so very much,
Master – anyone is able to call You.

*Amen.*

*All my discoveries have been*
*made in answer to prayer.*
– Isaac Newton

# SEEKING GOD FIRST

*"Your heavenly Father already knows all your needs. Seek the Kingdom of God above all else, and live righteously, and He will give you everything you need."*

~ MATTHEW 6:32-33 NLT

Dear Father God, may our prayers never seem to You like a huge shopping list. This is never our intention. We really desire to know the things of Your kingdom, and this will only come about through diligent and effective prayer.

*Amen.*

*God's chief gift to those who seek Him is Himself.*
– Edward Pusey

# SPEND TIME WITH GOD

*Delight yourself also in the LORD, and He shall give you the desires of your heart.*

~ PSALM 37:4

Heavenly Father, we have found that this beautiful Scripture verse is so very applicable to us when we spend lots of time in Your presence praying! The absolute delight of our hearts becomes a reality because we pray according to Your perfect will and not our will.

*Amen.*

*Genuine prayer will be looking out for answers.*
– William Plumber

# FAITH-FILLED PRAYER

*"You can pray for anything, and if you have faith, you will receive it."*

~ MATTHEW 21:22 NLT

Father God, prayers without faith
are worthless! Please increase our
faith to believe what we are praying.
The opposite prayer of fear is the
earnest prayer of faith. We have
witnessed the answer to those
faith-filled prayers many times before.
Please do it again, Master!

 *Amen.*

*What can be more excellent than prayer;
what is more profitable to our life;
what sweeter to our souls; what more
sublime, in the course of our whole
life, than the practice of prayer!*
– Saint Augustine

# STEADFAST PRAYER

*Work hard and serve the Lord enthusiastically. Rejoice in our confident hope. Be patient in trouble, and keep on praying. When God's people are in need, be ready to help them.*

~ Romans 12:11-13 NLT

Lord Jesus, in these troubled times in which we are living, You are looking for steadfast prayer warriors. Those people who will just quietly and persistently get on with praying for the lost! Because ongoing and faithful prayer moves mountains.

*Amen.*

*Do not pray by heart but with the heart.*

# A SELFLESS PRAYER WARRIOR

*O Lord, according to all Your righteousness, I pray,
let Your anger and Your fury be turned away from
Your city Jerusalem.*

~ DANIEL 9:16

Father God, Your faithful and bold
servant Daniel was such a selfless
prayer warrior, not being concerned
about himself but only his people.
Help us too, Holy Spirit, to not pray
self-centered prayers, but to rather be
more outward-focused when praying.

— *Amen.* —

*A holy mouth is made by praying.*
– E. M. Bounds

# PRAYER OF THE RIGHTEOUS

*But the prayer of the upright is His delight.*

~ PROVERBS 15:8

Father, You delight in hearing the
prayer of Your upright children.
But the prayer of the wicked and
unrighteous man You will by no means
listen to. You love those who walk and
follow the truth. A person who prays
eloquent prayers out loud for all to
hear, but whose heart is far from You,
is wasting their time because their
prayers fall upon deaf ears.

*Amen.*

*The high road of prayer is self-examination.*
– Martyn Lloyd-Jones

# UNITED IN PRAYER

*They all met together and were constantly united in prayer.*

~ ACTS 1:14 NLT

Father, when we, Your children, are in one accord, that is when Your blessed Holy Spirit is found among us. That is when Your power is truly manifest. But when there is division and contention and arguing, there is no peace or anointing of Your blessed Holy Spirit. We very much desire to pray together in unity.

*Amen.*

*There has never been a spiritual awakening in any country or locality that did not begin in united prayer.*
– A. T. Pierson

# CLOSER TO GOD

*A prayer of Moses the man of God …*

*~ Psalm 90*

Father God, what an incredible
relationship Moses must have had
with You. Just to read this beautiful
prayer prayed by him in Psalm 90
tells it all. We, too, so desire to
be able to speak (pray) with You
as Your beloved servant did.

— *Amen.* —

*The Bible is a letter God has sent to us;*
*prayer is a letter we send to Him.*
– Matthew Henry

# PRAY FOR THE UNBELIEVER

*"My servant Job will pray for you, and I will ac-*
*cept his prayer on your behalf."*

~ JOB 42:8 NLT

Lord, You hear the prayer of Your son
Job and the prayers of those who
love You so much. We shall, like Job,
pray for those who do not know You
personally, Father, lest they travel to a
lost eternity forever. We will intercede
on their behalf as Jesus did for us.

 *Amen.*

*I live in the Spirit of prayer. I pray as*
*I walk about, when I lie down and when I*
*rise up. And the answers are always coming.*
– George Müller

# IMPOSSIBLE PRAYERS ANSWERED

*"Whatever things you ask when you pray, believe that you receive them, and you will have them."*

~ MARK 11:24

Heavenly Father, we thank You for this extremely powerful Scripture verse that says we can pray for anything and if we believe that we've received it, it will be ours. The potential in this Bible promise from Jesus is endless. All we ask, Father, is to please increase our faith to believe You for the impossible.

— *Amen.* —

*Beyond our utmost wants His love and power can bless; to praying souls He always grants more than they can express.*

– John Newton

# GOD UNDERSTANDS

*He is despised and rejected by men, a Man of sorrows and acquainted with grief.*

~ ISAIAH 53:3

O dear Lord Jesus, You surely do understand what we are going through here on earth, because You have walked this road before us and have experienced all the pain and suffering we are going through at present. Thank You for not only rejoicing with us when we succeed, but also weeping with us when we are hurting.

*Amen.*

*There is nothing quite so comforting than talking with a person who has been there before us.*

# GOD-CENTERED

*I have not stopped thanking God for you. I pray for you constantly.*

~ EPHESIANS 1:16 NLT

Father God, even as Your great
apostle Paul prayed for Your people,
we too must never forget the
importance of praying for others.
So often our prayers are very selfish
and self-centered, like a shopping
list of personal wants. Forgive us,
Lord, and help us, we pray,
to be more God-centered.

*Amen.*

*When God intends great mercy for His
people, He first of all sets them praying.*
– Matthew Henry

# GETTING TO KNOW JESUS

*That I may know Him and the power of His resurrection, and the fellowship of His sufferings, being conformed to His death.*

~ PHILIPPIANS 3:10

Lord Jesus, the only way we will get to know someone very closely is to spend time talking with them. And, after all, that is exactly what prayer is, having a heart-to-heart talk with You! We so much desire to become better prayer warriors and by so doing, get to know You more intimately!

 *Amen.*

*Prayer is the link that connects us with God.*
– A. B. Simpson

# THE FAMILY UNIT

*... being heirs together of the grace of life, that your prayers may not be hindered.*

~ 1 PETER 3:7

Father God, we know how important marriage is to You and we also know that the family that prays together, stays together. Peter speaks about this very issue, saying that husbands and wives must give understanding to one another and compassion, so that their prayers will be answered. Help us, Master, to love each other much more than what we are doing at present.

— *Amen.* —

*A heap of unmeaning words only smothers the words of devotion.*

– J. Hamilton

# PRAYER AND FASTING

*So He said to them, "This kind can come out by nothing but prayer and fasting."*

~ MARK 9:29

Father, when it is a desperate and extremely serious situation, prayer and fasting are needed. Please help us to exercise much more discipline in our lives when seeking specific answers or decisions. You always answer the prayer of sincerity.

— *Amen.* —

*If I fail to spend two hours in prayer each morning, the devil gets the victory through the day.*
– Martin Luther

# PRAY MORE, WORRY LESS

*Be anxious for nothing, but in everything by prayer and supplication, with thanksgiving, let your requests be made known to God.*

~ PHILIPPIANS 4:6

Father, the more we pray and speak with You, the less anxious we will be. We know that a lot of our physical sickness comes from being worried and afraid of circumstances in our lives. We will choose to pray more and worry less.

*Amen.*

*It is strange that in our praying we seldom ask for a change of character, but always a change in circumstances.*

# HOUR OF PRAYER

*Now Peter and John went up together to the temple at the hour of prayer, the ninth hour.*

~ ACTS 3:1

Father God, prayer is a wonderful habit to keep, no matter what time it happens to be, but to do it regularly is so very important. And because of Peter and John's faithfulness, Jesus, You used them to perform a truly great miracle – the divine healing of a lame man. Help us to also be faithful and steadfast in our prayer life.

*Amen.*

*In seasons of distress and grief,*
*my soul has often found relief,*
*and oft escaped the tempter's snare*
*by thy return, sweet hour of prayer!*
– W. Walford

# THE IMPORTANCE OF PRAYER

*But we will give ourselves continually to prayer and to the ministry of the word.*

~ ACTS 6:4

---

Lord Jesus, what a very solemn reminder this is of the great importance of spending dedicated time in prayer! So much so that the twelve disciples separated themselves from the others for the very purpose of prayer. Forgive us, Father, for often not making prayer of the utmost importance in our lives.

 *Amen.*

---

*Prayer is not a form of employment or work; it is a complete lifestyle!*

# THE PRAYER OF FAITH

*Whenever I pray, I make my requests for all of you with joy.*

~ PHILIPPIANS 1:4 NLT

Father God, we continue to pray for our loved ones, especially those who have yet to meet with You personally. We pray with much joy because we pray the prayer of faith, and we believe that You hear each one of our prayers. And so, by faith, those we pray for will come to full salvation. Hallelujah!

*Amen.*

*Prayer without faith! What sort of prayer is it? It is the prayer of a man who does not believe in God.*
– Charles Spurgeon

# HEAR MY PRAYER

*Hear my prayer, O Lord, and let my cry come to You.*

~ Psalm 102:1

Father, what a desperate call this is.
How many times have we called
out to You in desperation as well?
But the wonderful news is that You
always hear our cry, no matter what
time of day or night it might be.
And no matter where that desperate
prayer is prayed – in a hospital or at
the scene of a road accident – You
always hear our prayer and for that,
Jesus, we are so very grateful.

— *Amen.* —

*God tells us to burden Him
with whatever burdens us.*

# GOD IS LISTENING

*The LORD is far from the wicked, but He hears the prayer of the righteous.*

~ PROVERBS 15:29

Master, thank You for hearing
our prayers. We are not fit, in our
own strength and goodness,
to approach You. But through the
precious blood of Christ, we are
cleansed and can offer our prayers
to You with confidence, knowing that
You hear them all. Thank You, Lord.

— *Amen.* —

*I always feel there is something
wrong if I go without prayer for
even half an hour in the day.*
– Charles Spurgeon

# PRAYER FOR REVIVAL

*O LORD, I have heard Your speech and was afraid;*
*O LORD, revive Your work in the midst of the years!*
~ HABAKKUK 3:2

Dearest Father God, please revive us,
Your fearful children. We do not
deserve another visitation from
You but please, we pray, for Your
own name's sake, revive Your
people yet once again, before the
second coming of Jesus Christ.

*Amen.*

*To ask in the name of Christ is …*
*to set aside our own will and*
*bow to the perfect will of God.*
– A. W. Pink

# EARNEST PRAYER

*"I have heard your prayer, I have seen your tears."*
~ Isaiah 38:5

Father God, You are really so very
kind and forgiving. When we earnestly
call upon You, we are never ever
in the slightest bit disappointed.
Even as You gave King Hezekiah
an extra fifteen years when he
was dying, so You will give us added
grace if we genuinely seek You.

*Amen.*

*I am convinced in my heart that
there is nothing in this world as
powerful as an earnest prayer.*

## STICK WITH JESUS

*"I know your works. See, I have set before you an open door, and no one can shut it; for you have a little strength, have kept My word, and have not denied My name."*

~ REVELATION 3:8

Sweet Jesus, we never want to ever deny Your beautiful name. We also, by Your grace, shall keep Your Holy Word, where all creation seems to want to compromise the Bible at every opportunity. We pray, Lord, strengthen us for this last chapter before You come again in all Your glory.

 *Amen.*

*We talk about heaven being so far away. It is within speaking distance to those who belong there.*
– Dwight Moody

# GOD IS WITH YOU

*When Your people go out to battle against their enemy, wherever You send them, and when they pray to the LORD …*

~ 1 KINGS 8:44

Father, what an incredible
answer to prayer, made by Your
servant Solomon. God, You said that
wherever Your people go, You will
hear our honest prayers and You
will go with us. Nothing has changed.
You are still the very same God. Please,
this day, hear our prayers, Father God.

*Amen.*

*The hand of faith never knocked in
vain at the door of heaven. Mercy is as
surely ours as if we had it, if we have
but faith and patience to wait for it.*
– William Burkitt

# JULY

*The Way of Peace*

# ABSOLUTE PEACE

*"Peace I leave with you, My peace I give to you; not as the world gives do I give to you. Let not your heart be troubled, neither let it be afraid."*

~ JOHN 14:27

Dear Father, I never really experienced absolute peace in my heart until I personally met Jesus Christ! We pray today that the countless troubled hearts in this world will meet Your precious Son, like we have, and will never be troubled again.

*Amen.*

*Peace is the deliberate adjustment of my life to the will of God.*

# BE A PEACEMAKER

*"Blessed are the peacemakers, for they shall be called the sons of God."*

~ MATTHEW 5:9

Father God, You do not say,
blessed are the peace lovers, but
rather blessed are the peacemakers!
We know that peace lovers will do
anything for a bit of peace. They are
completely self-centered and
are not concerned about others.
But peacemakers will give up all of their
own peace and security for those who
are traumatized and need peace.

— *Amen.* —

*Peace is not to be purchased
by the sacrifice of truth.*
– John Calvin

# THE FRUIT OF PEACE

*The Holy Spirit produces this kind of fruit in our lives: love, joy, peace, patience, kindness, goodness, faithfulness.*

~ GALATIANS 5:22 NLT

Master, with deep peace in
our hearts, the whole world can
see that we are, in fact, Your very
own children. Thank You for putting
that peace in our hearts from
the time we surrendered our lives
completely to Your lordship. We are
grateful for Your blessed peace.

*Amen.*

*Peace and comfort can be found
nowhere except in simple obedience.*
– François Fénelon

# HEAVENLY PEACE

*"In Me you may have peace. In the world you will have tribulation; but be of good cheer, I have overcome the world."*

~ JOHN 16:33

Father God, You never said that You would take us out of the world, but You have promised Your children that You would walk with us through the fire. And that we would have Your holy peace with us at all times. In times of trouble we can still have Your peace and for that we thank You, Father.

*Amen.*

*As we pour out our bitterness,*
*God pours in His peace.*
– F. B. Meyer

# SHARING PEACE

*To all who are in Rome, beloved of God, called to be saints: Grace to you and peace from God our Father and the Lord Jesus Christ.*

~ ROMANS 1:7

Father, what a wonderful greeting
from Your special apostle, Paul.
We pray that we, too, can convey
that peace to others when we meet
them in the workplace, at school,
or even on the sports field, never being
ashamed of the name of Jesus Christ.

*Amen.*

*He that is not a son of
peace is not a son of God.*
– Richard Baxter

# A LIFE OF PEACE

*Now may the God of peace be with you all.*
~ ROMANS 15:33

Father, this Bible verse describes You
so beautifully – "the God of peace."
Because that is exactly who You are!
Our prayer is that we, Your sons
and daughters, will also display
the peace of God in and through
our lifestyles daily, especially in our
meeting and greeting of one another.
—— *Amen.* ——

*Peace is not real peace until it
has been tested in the storm.*
– Eric Hayman

# PEACE WITH GOD

*This is the message of Good News for the people of Israel – that there is peace with God through Jesus Christ, who is Lord of all.*

~ ACTS 10:36 NLT

Heavenly Father, You sent us Your only begotten Son, Jesus Christ, and He came preaching peace. "Shalom" was His greeting every time He entered a home. Holy Spirit, please empower us to do likewise, to bring the spirit of peace wherever we travel in this world.

— *Amen.* —

*True peace comes when one is totally obedient to God's Holy Word.*

# EXTEND HIS PEACE

*"Behold, I will extend peace to her like a river."*

~ Isaiah 66:12

Father God, even as You extend Your beautiful peace to Jerusalem, we say thank You very much! May we also extend Your peace to a very fearful and troubled world. May the folk around us know that You have not abandoned them in any way and may we be Your witnesses to that fact.

*Amen.*

*The Christian needs to walk in peace,*
*so no matter what happens they will be*
*able to bear witness to a watching world.*

# KEEPING THE PEACE

*"First be reconciled to your brother, and then come and offer your gift."*

~ Matthew 5:24

Lord Jesus, sometimes it is very hard to make peace with those who are so near and dear to us because we love them so much. They hurt us without even knowing it. Help us to rise above our own selfish feelings, to forgive them unconditionally and to make our peace with them.

*Amen.*

*If thou wouldst find much favor and peace with God and man, be very low in thine own eyes. Forgive thyself little and others much.*
– Robert Leighton

# GOD'S LOVE BRINGS PEACE

*Therefore, having been justified by faith, we have peace with God through our Lord Jesus Christ.*

~ Romans 5:1

O Master, what peace this Scripture verse brings to our very souls. We are not in any circumstance justified and made worthy by our own doing. No, it's all because of what You did for us on the cross. Thank You, Lord, for the peace we have in You.

*Amen.*

*He did it all and what peace that brings to a lost soul.*

# THE PRINCE OF PEACE

*For God is not the author of confusion but of peace.*
*~ 1 CORINTHIANS 14:33*

Father God, we have never before
seen the absolute confusion that
we are seeing in the world today.
We know without a doubt that Satan
himself is the author of confusion.
But we also know that You alone
are the Author of total peace.
In fact, You are the Prince of
Peace and we worship You.

——— *Amen.* ———

*Peace is to the soul what health is to*
*the body: a sign of balance and order.*

# THE KEY TO PEACE

*For He Himself is our peace.*

~ EPHESIANS 2:14

Heavenly Father, as Paul says, we who were once far off have now been brought near by the blood of Christ (see Ephesians 2:13). Thank You, Lord Jesus, for giving us such peace through the knowledge that You have done it all, paid in full for all our sin and rebellion. What assurance that brings to our very souls!

— *Amen.* —

*Irrespective of how high the waves at sea might be, with Jesus in my rowboat, I'm at peace.*

# FEELING GOD'S PEACE

*The peace of God, which surpasses all understanding, will guard your hearts and minds through Christ Jesus.*

~ PHILIPPIANS 4:7

Father God, many times when Your pure and comforting peace comes upon us, we cannot understand it, we cannot explain it, but we can undeniably feel it in our hearts. We may be on an operating table in a hospital or speaking to a huge crowd in a stadium, but when we feel Your peace, it's amazing.

 — *Amen.* —

*A great many people are trying to make peace, but that has already been done. God has not left it for us to do; all we have to do is to enter into it.*
– Dwight Moody

# SPEAKING PEACE

*Grace to you and peace from God our Father and the Lord Jesus Christ.*

~ COLOSSIANS 1:2

Father, as Paul the apostle greets fellow believers, we too want to greet others in the same way. It's the peace and authority that we have when we greet others in Your holy name. No matter who we speak to – it might be a little child or the president of a nation – it still has the same impact, full of love, grace and peace. Help us to speak words of grace and peace.

*Amen.*

*To be of a peaceable spirit brings peace along with it.*
– Thomas Watson

# FINDING PEACE

*Then He arose and rebuked the wind, and said to the sea, "Peace, be still!" And the wind ceased and there was a great calm.*

~ MARK 4:39

Lord Jesus, sometimes we call You our Weatherman because we have seen the weather obey You and a potential disaster turn into a peaceful situation. You created the weather and we glorify You as we see Your power and might demonstrated through it.

*Amen.*

*If God be our God,*
*He will give us peace in trouble.*
– Thomas Watson

# THE NARROW GATE

*To guide us to the path of peace.*

~ LUKE 1:79 NLT

Father, if ever we needed to watch our step it is now, in these evil days in which we are living. You have even told us that the way to eternal death is wide and there are many who walk on that road. However, the road to eternal life is narrow, difficult, steep and not many walk in it. But it is the only way if we are looking for peace.

— *Amen.* —

*All men desire peace, but very few desire those things that make for peace.*

– Thomas à Kempis

# A SPIRIT OF PEACE

*Now the fruit of righteousness is sown in peace by those who make peace.*

~ JAMES 3:18

Father God, please help us to always operate in a spirit of peace. There is so much anger and so much violence that the world is desperate for men and women of peace to sow fruits of righteousness, of truth and, most of all, the fruit of love. This is our time to plant peace wherever we go and whatever we do, for Your glory, Lord.

*Amen.*

*It is the religion of Jesus alone that can bring peace to a man.*
– François Fénelon

# JESUS' PEACE

*Grace to you and peace from Him who is and who was and who is to come.*

~ REVELATION 1:4

Dear Lord Jesus, what a beautiful reminder today for us that You are the Prince of Peace: yesterday, today and forevermore (see Hebrews 13:8 and Isaiah 9:6). You never change and for us, living in an everchanging world, it is so comforting to know. Holy Spirit, please help us to tell others about the peace that is found in You.

— *Amen.* —

*If our minds are stayed upon God,*
*His peace will rule the affairs entertained by*
*our minds. If, on the other hand, we allow*
*our minds to dwell on the cares of this world,*
*God's peace will be far from our thoughts.*
– Woodrow Kroll

# WISDOM LEADS TO PEACE

*Her ways are ways of pleasantness, and all her paths are peace.*

~ PROVERBS 3:17

Good day, Father, we love and
appreciate You so very much. We ask
that You give us, Your children, more
wisdom today, please. We know when
we do things our way, they never
work, but when we apply Your
wisdom to our lives, then we walk
in paths of joy and of peace.

— *Amen.* —

*No more doing things my way,*
*only His way truly works.*

# A PROMISE OF PEACE

*Then the L*ORD *said to Gideon, "Peace be with you;
do not fear, you shall not die."*

~ JUDGES 6:23

Father God, what a reassuring word
to Your servant Gideon. We take that
word into our very own hearts today.
We shall not fear any longer and we
know that we shall only die when
our time has come, not a day earlier
or later. Thank You for that promise;
it brings peace into our hearts.

— *Amen.* —

*The peace of the soul consists in an
absolute resignation to the will of God.*
– François Fénelon

# SCRIPTURES OF PEACE

*"For I know the thoughts that I think toward you,"*
*says the LORD, "thoughts of peace and not of evil,*
*to give you a future and a hope."*

~ JEREMIAH 29:11

Dear Father God,
what beautiful words! We thank
You for these words of love. Even as
we read the above Scripture verse,
it floods us with peace and security.
It reminds us that You are for us
and not against us. Hallelujah!
What hopeful news. With this kind
of support, nothing at all will hold
us back. Thank You, Father.

*— Amen. —*

*Peace does not dwell in*
*outward things, but within the soul.*
– François Fénelon

# LOVE AND PEACE

*Great peace have those who love Your law, and nothing causes them to stumble.*

~ PSALM 119:165

Father, we know only too well
that we are saved by grace
(undeserved lovingkindness)
and not by doing good works.
Still, Your laws have been put there
for good reason. If we love You,
then we will willingly obey Your
commandments, which will bring
peace and direction into our lives.

— *Amen.* —

*With complete consecration
comes perfect peace.*
– Watchman Nee

# LIFE AND PEACE

*"My covenant was with him, one of life and peace,*
*and I gave them to him that he might fear Me."*
~ MALACHI 2:5

Father, when You say, "that we might
fear You," we know that You are
so deserving of respect and honor.
You are so worthy of our awe
and worship. We gladly bow the knee
to You, for then we receive deep
peace and a fulfilled life. Our awesome
God, we thank and praise You.

*Amen.*

*The happy sequence culminating in*
*fellowship with God is penitence, pardon,*
*and peace – the first we offer, the second*
*we accept, and the third we inherit.*
– Charles Brent

# THE GOAL IS PEACE

*"The glory of this latter temple shall be greater than the former," says the* LORD *of hosts. "And in this place I will give peace," says the* LORD *of hosts.*
~ HAGGAI 2:9

Father God, what an incredible promise You've given us: The latter shall be greater than the former and You shall give us Your peace. So, no matter what happens in these last days here on earth, we, Your children, shall walk in total peace. Hallelujah!

*Amen.*

*Peace rules the day when*
*Christ rules the mind.*

# THE GOD OF PEACE

*The God of peace will soon crush Satan under your feet.*

~ ROMANS 16:20 NLT

Father God, when we see what
is taking place all over the world,
we simply say: Father, come and
do Your final work soon, please,
because people are suffering greatly.
We can see the signs of Your coming
everywhere. It is as if Satan is having
his last onslaught because he knows
when You return, he is done.

 *Amen.*

*I hear the words of love, I gaze upon
the blood, I see the mighty sacrifice,
and I have peace with God.*
– Horatius Bonar

# PEACEFUL UNITY

*Be joyful. Grow to maturity. Encourage each other. Live in harmony and peace. Then the God of love and peace will be with you.*

~ 2 Corinthians 13:11 NLT

Father, we realize that if we want to live together in peace, then we are going to have to be a people of one mind. We cannot live peaceably if there is continual discord among us. Holy Spirit, please help us to love each other and be kind to one another so that the world will see that we are different.

— *Amen.* —

*What peace can they have who are not at peace with God?*
– Matthew Henry

# PRAYING FOR PEACE

*Pray for the peace of Jerusalem: "May they prosper who love you."*

~ PSALM 122:6

Dear Father God, this Scripture verse comes with a request and a reward. You have asked us to pray for the peace of Jerusalem and You have also said there will be a handsome reward for those who have prayed! We love Your city and Your people, Father, and we are delighted to pray for it unconditionally.

— *Amen.* —

*Peace cannot be achieved through violence; it can only be attained through understanding.*
– Ralph Waldo Emerson

# THE WAY OF PEACE

*"There is no peace for the wicked," says the* L<small>ORD</small>.
~ I<small>SAIAH</small> 48:22 <small>NLT</small>

Father God, what a very powerful and sobering statement. There is no peace for the wicked. We have seen it so often, Master, that those who have done evil can't sleep at night, expecting to be caught at any moment. Or how a man being unfaithful to his wife is always on the lookout, hoping to not be exposed for his sin. Today, we pray for the wicked. May they find their way back to You and Your peace.

—— *Amen.* ——

*There is no kind of peace which may be purchased on the bargain counter.*
– Carey Williams

# GOD IS WITH YOU

*I will both lie down in peace, and sleep; for You alone, O L*ORD*, make me dwell in safety.*

~ PSALM 4:8

Father God, we lie down and we sleep
peacefully because we know that
in You we have complete safety. It is
You, heavenly Father, who promised
us that You will never leave us nor
forsake us (see Hebrews 13:5).
We sleep like babies in a mother's
arms because of Your promise.

*Amen.*

*The best tranquilizer is a clear conscience!*
– Benjamin Franklin

# FOCUS ON GOD

*You will keep him in perfect peace, whose mind is stayed on You, because he trusts in You.*

*~ ISAIAH 26:3*

Father, when we focus on You and on You alone, we experience that peace that surpasses all understanding. We ask and pray that we will not allow the cares of this troubled world to infringe on our daily time spent in Your presence. We want to seek You first each morning, Father. We trust You and love You.

 *Amen.*

*God cannot give us a happiness and peace apart from Himself, because it is not there. There is no such thing.*

– C. S. Lewis

# SALTY FOR GOD

*"Salt is good for seasoning. But if it loses its flavor, how do you make it salty again? You must have the qualities of salt among yourselves and live in peace with each other."*

~ MARK 9:50 NLT

Dear Lord Jesus, these are Your very own words, that we are to be salty, to stand up for truth and righteousness. When we obey this mandate, we shall experience great peace in our hearts. Once we have spoken truth in love, we have the peace of God in our hearts. Please help us, Lord.

— *Amen.* —

*When our lives are filled with peace, faith and joy, people will want to know what we have.*

# AUGUST
*A Joyful Heart*

# THE JOY OF THE LORD

*Don't be dejected and sad, for the joy of the L*ORD *is your strength!*

~ NEHEMIAH 8:10 NLT

Dear Father in heaven, what a true
and wonderful thing to know that
when we have Your joy in our heart,
it gives us incredible strength –
both physical and, more importantly,
spiritual strength – and that joy is found
in only one place, in You alone.

*Amen.*

*The Lord gives His people perpetual joy*
*when they walk in obedience to Him.*
– Dwight Moody

# LIVE IN JOY

*"So shall My word be that goes forth from My mouth ... it shall accomplish what I please. For you shall go out with joy, and be led out with peace; the mountains and the hills shall break forth into singing before you, and all the trees of the field shall clap their hands."*

~ Isaiah 55:11-12

Yes, indeed, beloved Father, Your Word
brings much joy into our hearts.
Even the very hills and mountains shall
break forth with singing before You!
The trees shall clap their hands,
O Master. To hear and to read
Your Holy Scriptures brings much
joy and peace to our souls.
Thank You for Your Holy Word.

*Amen.*

*Joy is the serious business of heaven.*
– C. S. Lewis

# LOST SOULS SAVED

*"The kingdom of heaven is like treasure hidden in a field, which a man found and hid; and for joy over it he goes and sells all that he has and buys that field."*

~ MATTHEW 13:44

Dearest Father, thank You for showing us just how wonderfully joyful it is when one sinner truly finds salvation. It is such a lovely thing to watch a lost soul find Jesus Christ as Lord and King in their lives. Guide us in being good witnesses for You, rejoicing together with You for every lost soul saved.

— *Amen.* —

*Holy joy is the oil to the wheels of our obedience.*
– Matthew Henry

# LEAP FOR JOY

*"Rejoice in that day and leap for joy! For indeed your reward is great in heaven."*

~ LUKE 6:23

Dearest Father in heaven, it would
be a great honor to be persecuted
for our faith in Your Son, Jesus Christ.
And we know that when You come
again to take us to heaven, You will
have no problem recognizing us
as Your faithful children. Help us
to be ready when You come.
Help us to rejoice in persecution,
knowing that You are faithful.

*Amen.*

*Christ is the desire of nations,
the joy of angels, the delight of the Father.*
– John Bunyan

# THE BOOK OF LIFE

*Jesus said, "Rejoice because your names are written in heaven."*

~ LUKE 10:20

Lord Jesus, it is always such a great honor to go out in Your name and to work for You, spreading the gospel and setting the captives free! But we need to always remember that You said this was all good, but most of all, we need to rejoice that our names are written in the Book of Life.

 *Amen.*

*Nothing can give it so much as the thought of His coming. There may be sorrow in the night, but joy enough – fulness of joy – in that morning when we shall see Him as He is.*
– G. V. Wigram

# THE FINISH LINE

*I have fought the good fight, I have finished the race, and I have remained faithful. And now the prize awaits me – the crown of righteousness, which the Lord, the righteous Judge, will give me on the day of His return.*

~ 2 TIMOTHY 4:7-8

Father God, it is all about finishing strong irrespective of how tough it may become. We are bound to meet many challenges along the way, even tribulations, but with great joy, we will not give up. Instead, we will press hard to the finish line for Jesus Christ. Please help us to remain steadfast and true.

— *Amen.* —

*Joy is at the heart of satisfied living.*
– J. I. Packer

# A JOYFUL WELCOME

*Zacchaeus quickly climbed down and took Jesus to his house in great excitement and joy.*

*~ LUKE 19:6 NLT*

Lord Jesus, Zacchaeus joyfully received You into his home! I earnestly pray that we, Your children, would give You the very same welcome in our lives and homes. Not only that, but Zacchaeus had a complete change of life forever. Master, we pray that would be our testimony too!

*Amen.*

*Take a saint, and put him into any condition, and he knows how to rejoice in the Lord.*
– Walter Cradock

# THE JOY OF A CHRISTIAN

*How we thank God for you! Because of you we
have great joy as we enter God's presence.*

~ 1 THESSALONIANS 3:9 NLT

Father God, we do really hope that
we bring joy to our fellow believers
when they observe our Christian
lifestyle. We pray that our faith will
encourage others to stand up and
be counted for Jesus. And not
only that, but to also rejoice in
our commitment to You alone.
We pray that our joy in You will be
an encouragement for them too.

*Amen.*

*May not a single moment of
my life be spent outside the light,
love and joy of God's presence.*
– Andrew Murray

# A HEART THAT REJOICES

*"Therefore you now have sorrow; but I will see you again and your heart will rejoice, and your joy no one will take from you."*

~ John 16:22

Precious Lord Jesus, what a great promise to look forward to; You coming in all Your splendor and power and glory. Indeed, what a great day that shall be, Master, full of joy and hope. But until then, we shall keep on going and be a blessing to as many people as we can, making You our only joy. Lord, take away from us all joy that does not come directly from You.

— *Amen.* —

*Seek to cultivate a buoyant, joyous sense of the crowded kindnesses of God in your daily life.*
– Alexander Maclaren

# FIXED ON HEAVEN

*Looking unto Jesus, the author and finisher of our faith, who for the joy that was set before Him endured the cross.*

~ Hebrews 12:2

Father, when we see the example of Your beloved Son, we realize that He was not focused on this fleeting life, which is over so quickly. No, He had His eyes fixed on eternity, and that brought Him great peace and joy in the midst of His affliction. May we, too, set our minds on things above.

— *Amen.* —

*The joy of the Christian is a holy joy;*
*the happiness of the Christian*
*is a serious happiness.*
– Martyn Lloyd-Jones

# THE SECRET TO JOY

*"I will rejoice in Jerusalem, and joy in My people."*
~ ISAIAH 65:19

Our Lord God, we, Your children,
are aware of how much You love
Jerusalem and how much You
love us, Your very own people.
So much so that You even gave Your
beloved Son for our sakes, so that we
might have eternal life. Holy Spirit,
even today, let us walk in obedience
to God's word over us, we pray.

— *Amen.* —

*Joy is the gigantic secret of the Christian.*
– G. K. Chesterton

# THE SOURCE OF JOY

*All the trees of the field are withered; surely joy has withered away from the sons of men.*

*~ JOEL 1:12*

Father God, there is nothing like a crop failure or an economic failure to erode the joy of the Lord in our lives! But, Lord, please empower us not to look to worldly situations as a source of our joy. We look to Jesus for our joy and to nothing else.

— *Amen.* —

*Joy is delight at God's grace,
which enables us to endure our trials.*

# JESUS' TRIUMPHANT RETURN

*And all the people went up after him; and the people played the flutes and rejoiced with great joy, so that the earth seemed to split with their sound.*

~ 1 Kings 1:40

Father God, what a great day
that must have been when King
Solomon was proclaimed king.
Oh, but Father, we cannot wait for
the day when Jesus, the true King,
returns to earth as Lord and Savior.
The utter joy we will experience
will be unimaginable!

*Amen.*

*True Christian joy is both
a privilege and a duty.*
– Jerry Bridges

# TIDINGS OF JOY

*The angel said to them, "Do not be afraid, for be-hold, I bring you good tidings of great joy which will be to all people."*

~ LUKE 2:10

Lord Jesus, what joy in all the earth
to hear the great, great news of Your
royal arrival on earth. To think of what
You sacrificed to leave Your majestic
throne in heaven to come to earth in
the form of a defenseless babe, we,
Your loved ones, say, "Thank You!"
We have no other words that are
good enough or sufficient!

*Amen.*

*We are meant to enjoy
our salvation, not endure it.*
– John Blanchard

# FROM SUFFERING TO JOY

*"You will be sorrowful, but your sorrow will be turned into joy."*

~ JOHN 16:20

Lord Jesus, You are reminding us that, much like a woman who is in pain while she gives birth to her child and whose suffering soon turns into ecstatic joy, it shall be like that at Your return to this sad world in which we are living at present. What a day that shall be, every knee shall bow and every tongue confess that You are Lord (see Philippians 2:10-11).

*Amen.*

*We never better enjoy ourselves than when we most enjoy God.*
– Benjamin Whichcote

# STRENGTHENED BY JOY

*Strengthened with all might, according to His glorious power, for all patience and longsuffering with joy.*

~ COLOSSIANS 1:11

Father God, we truly hope that You are also receiving good reports that our faith in Jesus and our love for the saints is standing strong. Our hope is that very soon we shall no longer have to wait for the return of Your blessed Son, King Jesus. But until that glorious day, please continue to strengthen us, we pray, with Your joy.

*Amen.*

*If you have no joy in your religion, there's a leak in your Christianity somewhere.*
– Billy Sunday

# SHOUTING WITH JOY

*Sing aloud to God our strength; make a joyful shout to the God of Jacob.*

~ PSALM 81:1

Father God, we really want to
repent and say sorry for not
expressing ourselves more verbally.
We do not shout out our great
love for You as we should.
You have done so much for us and
we should joyfully shout our praise.
We seem to have no problem shouting
out for our favorite sports team.
Help us to become a lot more openly
vocal about our love for You.

— *Amen.* —

*Next to Christ, I have but one joy,*
*the apple of the eye of my delights –*
*to preach Christ my Lord.*
– Samuel Rutherford

# THE BEST KIND OF JOY

*But none of these things move me; nor do I count my life dear to myself, so that I may finish my race with joy, and the ministry which I received from the Lord Jesus.*

~ ACTS 20:24

Heavenly Father, it is all about finishing the race and finishing it with joy! We are counting it a great privilege and joy to be part of the "end time" army of Jesus Christ. Holy Spirit, please, just like You did with the apostle Paul, enable us to finish strong.

— *Amen.* —

*Joy in God is the happiest of all joys.*
– Charles Spurgeon

# CHOOSING JOY

*And the disciples were filled with joy and with the Holy Spirit.*

~ ACTS 13:52

Father God, joy comes through
obedience and not cowering
down to peer pressure. Even as
Paul and Barnabas preached
the precious gospel to whoever
would listen, and were persecuted
for it, they counted it all joy and
were filled with the Holy Spirit.
So be it with us too, Master.

 *Amen.*

*Joy is not an accident of temperament
or an unpredictable providence;
joy is a matter of choice.*
– J. I. Packer

# COMING TOGETHER

*That I may come to you with joy by the will of God, and may be refreshed together with you.*

*~ ROMANS 15:32*

Father God, there is something
so refreshing to the soul of a man
when he meets with his brothers and
sisters in Christ. And that is why You
continue to remind us to meet often.
It is like iron sharpening iron, like Your
Word says (see Proverbs 27:17).
If we neglect meeting together,
we become dull and blunt. Please let
us not miss the opportunities we have
to meet with our fellow believers.

— *Amen.* —

*Nothing gives believers more joy
than to see God glorified.*
– R. C. Sproul

# WORK TOGETHER

*That does not mean we want to dominate you by telling you how to put your faith into practice. We want to work together with you so you will be full of joy, for it is by your own faith that you stand firm.*

~ 2 CORINTHIANS 1:24 NLT

Father God, forbid that we would ever lord it over our fellow believers! For we are just fellow workers for the gospel, like any other child of God. And our joy is to see them succeed in their individual works for the kingdom of God. Please help us to support others in their ministry.

*Amen.*

*We have been called as mature Christians to pass on the baton!*

# A CROWN OF JOY

*Therefore, my dear brothers and sisters, stay true to the Lord. I love you and long to see you, dear friends, for you are my joy and the crown I receive for my work.*

~ PHILIPPIANS 4:1 NLT

Father God, we too need to stand fast in the faith, which we are not ashamed to proclaim boldly. Lord Jesus, You did it so often for our sakes when You walked on the earth! We want to be Your joy and Your crown as we make a decision to live holy lives for You.

—— *Amen.* ——

*The test of Christian character should be that a man is a joy-bearing agent to the world.*
– Henry Ward Beecher

# REJOICE IN SAVED SOULS

*After all, what gives us hope and joy, and what will be our proud reward and crown as we stand before our Lord Jesus when He returns? It is you!*
~ 1 Thessalonians 2:19 nlt

Father God, we want to be more evangelically minded. We want to see more lost souls coming into the Kingdom before Your fast approaching return. It is such a joy to see souls truly saved. Holy Spirit, please use us more effectively to spread the Good News in these last days, we pray.

—— *Amen.* ——

*Your only joy is to be found in obeying Him.*
– Sinclair Ferguson

# THE KINGDOM OF JOY

*The kingdom of God is not eating and drinking, but righteousness and peace and joy in the Holy Spirit.*
~ ROMANS 14:17

Father God, this Scripture verse is such an accurate message for us today. We are in this world, but we are not of this world. Therefore, just as You have said, our lives are not to be taken up so much by eating and drinking, but rather by concentrating on the things of eternal value. Help us to demonstrate the righteousness, peace and joy that come from the Holy Spirit.

*Amen.*

*As representatives of the Lord, we need to focus more on the Maker and less on the bread and the water!*

# JOY IN THE MORNING

*Weeping may endure for a night, but joy comes in the morning.*

~ PSALM 30:5

Father, how we really know the full value of this Scripture verse, especially when we have been through great fiery trials in this life. First of all, we could never have endured them or even survived them without You walking with us. And secondly, we have only been able to find our joy again (in the morning) through Your lovingkindness. Thank You, Lord, that joy comes after sorrow and pain.

— *Amen.* —

*Keep your eyes open, your heart at peace and your soul in the joy of Christ.*
– Thomas Merton

# A HEART OF JOY

*My child, if your heart is wise, my own heart will rejoice!*

~ PROVERBS 23:15 NLT

Dearest Lord Jesus, we can wholeheartedly agree that a wise son brings much joy to his father and mother. And sadly, a foolish son also brings much shame upon his father and mother. We pray for our children and grandchildren, that they would not depart from the faith. Please keep them close to Yourself and help us to set a good example for them in our words and deeds.

*Amen.*

*A God-fearing child brings much honor to his parents.*

# WORK HARD FOR GOD

*God keeps him busy with the joy of his heart.*
~ ECCLESIASTES 5:20

Father God, You created us,
Your children, to work. It is an
honorable thing to work hard. And in
the same manner, an abominable
thing to be lazy as it brings no glory
to Jesus' name. We determine in
our hearts not to bring You shame,
Father, by not working hard.
Help us to recognize that work
is a privilege to be enjoyed.

*Amen.*

*Read the Bible.*
*Work hard and honestly.*
*And don't complain.*
– Billy Graham

# WHAT GREAT JOY!

*For I am not ashamed of the gospel of Christ, for it is the power of God to salvation for everyone who believes, for the Jew first and also for the Greek.*

~ ROMANS 1:16

Father God, we experience great joy and honor when we can verbalize our faith in Jesus Christ. It truly does something very special to our heart and soul. We pray for more courage, Master, to take every opportunity to speak up and not to hold back!

 *Amen.*

*If we do not speak up, the Bible tells us that the very rocks will (see Luke 19:40)!*

# REJOICE IN THE LORD

*... whose names are in the Book of Life. Rejoice in the Lord always. Again I will say, rejoice!*

~ PHILIPPIANS 4:3-4

Father, there is absolutely nothing else in this old world that will give us more joy than to know beyond any doubt that our names are written in the Lamb's Book of Life. And the proof of this wonderful miracle is found in Romans 10:9, which says: "If you confess with your mouth the Lord Jesus and believe in your heart that God has raised Him from the dead, you will be saved."

*Amen.*

*My name once stood with sinners lost, and bore a painful record; but by His blood the Savior crossed, and placed it on His roll.*

– D. S. Warner

# THE JOY OF REVIVAL

*And there was great joy in that city.*

~ ACTS 8:8

Father God, there is always great
joy when even one soul comes
to salvation. We know what it is like to
see revival; it is very humbling, but at
the same time extremely exciting.
When we watch, like silent spectators,
the Holy Spirit moving in power,
there is no joy that can compare.
Please use us for a revival we pray.

 *Amen.*

*Lord, I thank Thee that Thou has shown me*
*this marvelous working, though I was but an*
*adoring spectator rather than an instrument.*
– Robert Murray McCheyne

# THANK YOU, LORD!

*The pastures are clothed with flocks; the valleys also are covered with grain; they shout for joy, they also sing.*

~ PSALM 65:13

Father God, the land itself shouts
for joy, and sings what a mighty
and gracious God You are to us,
Your children. You always hear the
prayers of Your faithful children and,
even though we do not deserve it,
You still watch over us and bless
our fields, our crops and our work.
Thank You, Lord, we love You
and worship You in all things.

— *Amen.* —

*The Great Shepherd watches
over His sheep; He never sleeps.*

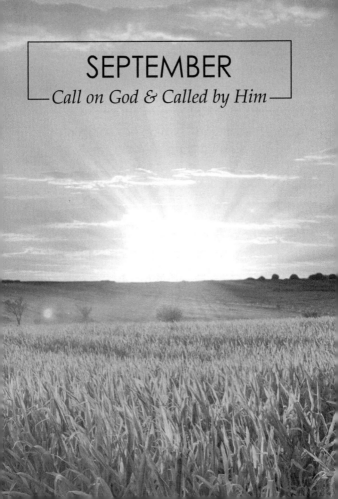

# SEPTEMBER
*Call on God & Called by Him*

# CALL ON GOD

*"Call to Me, and I will answer you, and show you*
*great and mighty things, which you do not know."*
~ Jeremiah 33:3

Father God, if we do not call upon
Your mighty name, how can we
expect answers to our questions
and solutions to our problems.
As the old saying goes, "If you do
not ask, you do not get." It is in
the asking that You, Lord, show us
great and awesome things.

— *Amen.* —

*When I pray, coincidences happen,*
*and when I don't, they don't.*
– William Temple

# GOD WILL DELIVER YOU

*"Call upon Me in the day of trouble; I will deliver you, and you shall glorify Me."*

~ Psalm 50:15

Heavenly Father, thank You that we may call upon You at any time for help, no matter how big or how small our problem might be. There are so many troubles in the world at the moment, Father, and yet we know that You are always there for us. We glorify Your name for always delivering us.

*Amen.*

*There is no trouble that is too big for Jesus to handle.*

# GOD WILL ANSWER

*"He shall call upon Me, and I will answer him; I will be with him in trouble; I will deliver him and honor him."*

~ PSALM 91:15

Father God, we experience such a comfort in knowing that You are always only a prayer away, especially when we are in trouble. We know that through great trials we grow stronger as we see how You help us in mighty and awesome ways. Thank You for always delivering us from trouble.

*Amen.*

*Trials teach us what we are; they dig up the soil and let us see what we are made of.*
– Charles Spurgeon

# PRAY MORE, WAIT MORE

*"Then you will call upon Me and go and pray to Me, and I will listen to you."*

~ JEREMIAH 29:12

Father in heaven, we bless and thank You for such an encouraging Scripture verse. We need to do less and pray more. Please forgive us, Lord, for calling upon You in prayer and, before You graciously have an opportunity to answer us, we go ahead and make our own plan, which never works anyway. Please help us to wait patiently before we act.

 *Amen.*

*Cast your troubles where you have cast your sins.*
– Charles Spurgeon

# A MORNING PRAYER

*Then early in the morning all the people came to Him in the temple to hear Him.*

~ LUKE 21:38

Father, we know that the early bird catches the worm. Oftentimes Your Son could not be found by His disciples because He had risen very early in the morning and was up on the mountain praying to You. Help us to start the day with You, knowing that You will be with us the whole day through.

*Amen.*

*In the morning, prayer is the key that opens to us the treasures of God's mercies and blessings.*
– Billy Graham

# CALLING ON HIS NAME

*Moses and Aaron were among His priests, and Samuel was among those who called upon His name; they called upon the Lord, and He answered them.*

~ Psalm 99:6

Father, no matter who we might be,
just ordinary common folk, if we call
upon You in all sincerity, then You
answer us just like You answered
the mighty Bible prophets of old.
Please forgive us for not calling upon
Your beautiful name more often.

— *Amen.* —

*All who call on God in true faith,
earnestly from the heart, will certainly
be heard, and will receive what
they have asked and desired.*
– Martin Luther

# A CALL IN TROUBLE

*Do not hide Your face from me in the day of my trouble; incline Your ear to me; in the day that I call, answer me speedily.*

~ PSALM 102:2

Heavenly Father, in this Scripture verse we hear the desperate call of a man in deep distress. And in this world today there is just so much fear and anxiety among people. Please show us how to really comfort Your people, Lord. Please help us to help others.

— *Amen.* —

*All my discoveries have been made in answer to prayer.*
– Isaac Newton

# ONE PRAYER AWAY

*Because He has inclined His ear to me, therefore I will call upon Him as long as I live.*

~ PSALM 116:2

Father God, we are so very grateful that You are always so available to listen to us when we call out to You. And, Father, just as the psalmist said, because You are so very willing to incline Your ear towards us, Your children, we feel that You are only one prayer away.

 *Amen.*

*My prayer today is that God would make me an extraordinary Christian.*
– George Whitefield

# TO ALL WHO CALL ON HIM

*The LORD is near to all who call upon Him, to all who call upon Him in truth. He will fulfill the desire of those who fear Him; He also will hear their cry and save them.*

*~ PSALM 145:18-19*

Father, You are holy, and to be feared
and respected. We approach Your
throne with reverence. Thank You
for hearing our cries and for saving
us from trouble. Please forgive
us for selfish prayers that do not
please You. Help us to call upon
You in truth only, we pray.

— *Amen.* —

*We have the truth and we
need not be afraid to say so.*
– J. C. Ryle

# WHOEVER CALLS
# ON THE LORD

*"I will call them My people, who were not My people, and her beloved, who was not beloved."*

~ ROMANS 9:25

---

Father God, we just love You so very much, especially the way in which You are no respecter of persons. Romans 10:13 says, *"whoever calls on the name of the LORD shall be saved."* Thank You, Father, that You will not turn away anyone who sincerely calls upon Your lovely name.

*Amen.*

---

*Faith is the evidence of divine adoption.*
– John Calvin

# O LORD, HEAR AND FORGIVE!

*"O Lord, hear! O Lord, forgive! O Lord, listen and act! Do not delay for Your own sake, my God, for Your city and Your people are called by Your name."*

~ DANIEL 9:19

Father, even as Daniel pleaded
with You to save Your people
and Jerusalem, we too need
You now like never ever before.
Please undertake for us, for there
are so many ungodly acts taking
place in the world and many are
blindly following after them. We call
on You to help us and protect us.

— *Amen.* —

*Keep the truth and the truth will keep you.*
– William Bridge

# HE PATIENTLY LISTENS

*Be merciful to me, O Lord, for I cry to You all day long.*

~ Psalm 86:3

O Lord, You never tire of hearing our prayers. You never stop listening when we constantly cry out to You about the troubles and concerns that weigh heavy on our hearts. You are so good, so ready to forgive, so full of unfailing love for all who ask for Your help. Thank You for listening and for answering in Your perfect timing.

— *Amen.* —

*Prayer is the way and means God has appointed for the communication of the blessings of His goodness to His people.*
– A. W. Pink

# A HEART ON FIRE

*"But why do you call Me 'Lord, Lord,' and not do the things which I say?"*

~ Luke 6:46

Dear Lord Jesus, these are very strong words from You to us. You clearly have no time whatsoever for hypocrites! You said in Revelation 3:16 that if we be lukewarm, You would vomit us out of Your mouth. Master, we desire to be red hot for You. Let us not be guilty of calling on You with a heart that is not on fire for You.

*Amen.*

*With Jesus Christ there can be no half measures; it's all or nothing.*

# REPRESENTATIVES OF GOD

*Called to be saints, with all who in every place call on the name of Jesus Christ our Lord, both theirs and ours.*

~ 1 CORINTHIANS 1:2

Father God, we have an obligation to be representatives of Your only Son, our Savior Jesus Christ. We are by no means ashamed to call upon His name wherever we go. We really desire to be a good testimony of His life worked through us. We not only call *on* You in prayer but are called *by* You to be Your witnesses on earth. Please help us in this task.

 *Amen.*

*Every Christian occupies some kind of pulpit and preaches some kind of gospel.*

# HEAR GOD'S CALL

*The LORD came and stood and called as at other times, "Samuel! Samuel!" And Samuel answered, "Speak, for Your servant hears."*

~ 1 SAMUEL 3:10

Father, forbid that when You call us,
we do not hear Your beautiful voice.
In these last days in which we
are living, where things seem to
be so terribly urgent, we cannot
afford to miss the call. Lord, please
help us to be extra sensitive to hear
Your call and to answer You.

*Amen.*

*Let us open our spiritual ears to hear
the still small voice of God calling.*

# SHARE THE GOOD NEWS

*He first found his own brother Simon, and said to him, "We have found the Messiah" (which is translated, the Christ).*

~ JOHN 1:41

Father God, it was Andrew whom You called and used to introduce Peter to Jesus. And that is why Andrew, Peter's brother, is so often known as the "introducer", because he introduced Peter to the Messiah. We, too, have been called to tell others about You. Please help us to share this wonderful, life-changing news with others.

 *Amen.*

*Christ is the final word about salvation.*
*Here He is not only without peer,*
*He is without a competitor.*
– G. Campbell Morgan

# CALLED TO BE EQUAL

*God has shown me that I should no longer think of anyone as impure or unclean.*

~ Acts 10:28 NLT

Dearest Father God, this Scripture verse reminds us that if a person acknowledges Jesus as their Savior, then that person is our brother or sister in Christ irrespective of their color, creed or culture. Please help us to never show partiality. Help us to remember that we have all been called by You and we are all equal in Your sight.

— *Amen.* —

*All men are created equal, it is only men themselves who place themselves above equality.*

# CALLED BY NAME

*"Fear not, for I have redeemed you; I have called
you by your name; You are Mine."*

~ ISAIAH 43:1

Father, we become quite emotional
when we even think that You, the
Creator of heaven and earth, know
each one of us by name! You have
called us by name to follow You
and You know us. To think that
we, little specs of dust in a great
universe, are known by name.
Oh, how we love You, Abba Father.

*Amen.*

*To be known by one's first name
is such an intimate thing!*

# CALLED TO REPENTANCE

*"But go and learn what this means: 'I desire mercy and not sacrifice.' For I did not come to call the righteous, but sinners, to repentance."*

~ MATTHEW 9:13

Father God, we love You so much for this very reason, for the fact that You love and call sinners! Just as we were in sin, Your Son, Jesus Christ, gave up His life so that we can be saved and made righteous. Father, forbid that we would ever take this great gift for granted.

 *Amen.*

*We are not saved by our giving;*
*we are saved by God's giving.*
– A. W. Pink

# CALLED ON TIME

*"The Teacher has come and is calling for you."*

~ JOHN 11:28

Father, when we hear that Your
blessed Son, Jesus, is calling for us,
it's a divine moment in time!
For Jesus Christ is never late and He
is never early; He is always on time.
And just like in the case of Mary
and Martha, when their brother
Lazarus had died, Jesus arrived to
raise him from the dead right on time.
Please help us to trust Your timing and
be ready to respond when You call us.

— *Amen.* —

*Be prepared and ready for the call.*

# CALLED TO OBEY

*But the Angel of the LORD called to him from heaven and said, "Abraham, Abraham!" So he said, "Here I am."*

~ GENESIS 22:11

Father, You must have been pleased to see the extent of Abraham's obedience to Your call. You tested his amazing faith by asking him to sacrifice Isaac, his son whom he patiently waited to receive. You have called us to obey You and we pray that we will be wholehearted in our obedience to You.

*Amen.*

*Believing and obeying always run side by side.*
– Charles Spurgeon

# CALLED TO BE HOLY

*But as He who called you is holy, you also be holy in all your conduct.*

~ 1 PETER 1:15

Father, please forgive us for so many times forgetting that You are a holy God and therefore cannot look upon sin of any description. We need to pray and to live with much more humility, especially when we tell folk in the world that we are Your own representatives! You have called us to be holy as You are holy.

 *Amen.*

*Take time to be holy, speak oft with thy Lord; abide in Him always, and feed on His Word.*
– William Longstaff

# CALLED TO PEACE

*But God has called us to peace.*

~ 1 CORINTHIANS 7:15

Father God, this particular verse is so important in the marriage and home situation. And, Father, if ever we needed peace and reconciliation in our homes and marriages, it's now! Let us be peacemakers and work things out with love and patience. You have called us to peace so please help us to live in peace.

*Amen.*

*Grace is the free favor of God; peace is the condition which results from its reception.*
– H. L. Goudge

# CALLED BY A NEW NAME

*God said to him, "Your name is Jacob; your name shall not be called Jacob anymore, but Israel shall be your name." So He called his name Israel.*

~ Genesis 35:10

Father God, it is such an
honor and a great blessing
to be given a brand-new name.
In fact, once we are born again,
we take a completely
new character altogether.
Yes, indeed, we become
new creations and are called
by a new name. Hallelujah!

— *Amen.* —

*When we are born again, a new life – the life of God – is put into us by the Holy Spirit.*

– F. B. Meyer

# CALLED TO DO GOD'S WILL

*Now when Jesus looked at him, He said, "You are Simon the son of Jonah. You shall be called Cephas" (which is translated, A Stone).*

~ JOHN 1:42

Father, what an amazing call to a man who eventually led the first church and then died the death of a martyr. There is hope for each and every one of us. Father, please use us in any way that will bring glory to the name of Your only Son, Jesus Christ our Lord. At the end of the day, it is all about You, Lord Jesus, and nothing else.

— *Amen.* —

*Our high and privileged calling is to do the will of God in the power of God for the glory of God.*

– J. I. Packer

# CALLED TO BE WISE

*Wisdom cries aloud, "I call to you, to all of you! I raise my voice to all people."*

~ PROVERBS 8:4 NLT

Heavenly Father, if there is one thing that we need, it is wisdom. Please forgive us for so often being stubborn and for trying to do things on our own. Our plans never work, and then we tend to come crying to You asking what has happened to us and to please rescue us. Please help us to heed Wisdom's call, we pray.

*Amen.*

*The wisest person in the world is the person who knows the most about God.*
– A. W. Tozer

# CALLED TO SERVE

*"You call Me Teacher and Lord, and you say well, for so I am."*

~ JOHN 13:13

Lord Jesus, we call You Lord
and Teacher. You are everything to
us and we desire more than anything
else to obey You in every area of
our lives. Even as You so lovingly
wash our dirty feet, we desire to do
just the same for our fellow man.
What a great mentor and example
You are to us all, Master!

*Amen.*

*God is not greater if you reverence Him,*
*but you are greater if you serve Him.*
– Saint Augustine

# CALLED INTO EXISTENCE

*God called the light Day, and the darkness He called Night. So the evening and the morning were the first day.*

~ GENESIS 1:5

Our blessed Father God, Creator of all things, You just spoke the word and everything was created. What an incredible and most powerful God You are. Please forgive us, Your children, for not always treating You with the honor and respect You deserve. You called everything into existence and we are Yours.

 *Amen.*

*Bring me a worm that can comprehend a man, and then I will show you a man that can comprehend the Triune God.*
– John Wesley

# CALLED OUT OF DARKNESS

*But you are a chosen generation, a royal priest-hood, a holy nation, His own special people, that you may proclaim the praises of Him who called you out of darkness into His marvelous light.*

~ 1 PETER 2:9

Dear heavenly Father, we praise and thank You for calling us out of the darkness of sin, death and separation from You. Without You there is no light and what a terrible place to be. Thank You that we can walk in the light of Your glory and grace.

—— *Amen.* ——

*Glory in Christ and you can bask in His light forever.*
– Woodrow Kroll

# THE FINAL CALL

*You do not know what will happen tomorrow. For what is your life? It is even a vapor that appears for a little time and then vanishes away.*

~ JAMES 4:14

Father, You have called us to love and serve You. You have called us to follow where You lead and to tell others about You. But the final and most significant call You make is the call for us to go home to our eternal home in heaven. We pray, Father, that we will be ready and waiting when You call us home.

 *Amen.*

*When His chosen ones shall gather to their home beyond the skies, and the roll is called up yonder, I'll be there.*

– James Black

# OCTOBER
*The God of Miracles*

# THE MIRACLE OF NEW LIFE

*Jesus answered and said to him, "Most assuredly, I say to you, unless one is born again, he cannot see the kingdom of God."*

~ JOHN 3:3

Father God, without any doubt the greatest miracle of all is when a person is born again. This can only happen through Your power and the work of the Holy Spirit. King Jesus, when a broken man, who has lost everything, finds You and starts a new life, it truly is a miracle. We praise You for the miracle of new life in You!

— *Amen.* —

*There is nothing more beautiful than to see new birth in Christ!*

# PRAY BY FAITH

*So Jesus answered and said to him, "What do you want Me to do for you?"*

~ MARK 10:51

O Master, there are so many people who are so desperate for a miracle in their lives. Looking at a blind man, You asked a strange question: "What do you want Me to do for you?" Bartimaeus answered correctly: "Rabboni, that I may receive my sight." And he was healed instantly. Lord, help us to have the faith to tell You what we require.

— *Amen.* —

*Prayer honors God, acknowledges His being, exalts His power, adores His providence, secures His aid.*
– E. M. Bounds

# THE MIRACLE WORKER

*Do not be afraid. Stand still, and see the salvation of the LORD.*

~ EXODUS 14:13

Heavenly Father, what an incredible
miracle that must have been
to see: a sea parting and an entire
nation passing through on dry land;
then Pharaoh's army chasing hard from
behind, being totally drowned as the
sea closes over them. We praise You,
our mighty miracle-working God!

*Amen.*

*That we must love one God only
is a thing so evident that it does
not require miracles to prove it.*

– Blaise Pascal

# JESUS WEPT

*Then Jesus shouted, "Lazarus, come out!"*
~ JOHN 11:43 NLT

Father God, after four days in
the tomb, in a hot climate, the body
should have been decomposing,
but it did not. In fact, at the command
of Your Son, Jesus, the body rose
from the dead and came forth.
Father, we praise You for not only
being a miraculous God, but also a
very loving and compassionate God.

— *Amen.* —

*Jesus wept when He saw the despair
of Lazarus's family (see John 11:35)!*

# 5,000 MEN FED

*Now those who had eaten the loaves were about five thousand men.*

~ Mark 6:44

Father, what a great encouragement to see over five thousand hungry men fed with two small fish and five small barley loaves of bread. You are indeed a miracle-working God and we believe in You with all our hearts. Please help us never to doubt Your power and ability.

*Amen.*

*Faith sees the invisible,*
*believes the unbelievable,*
*and receives the impossible.*
– Corrie ten Boom

# SIMPLE FAITH

*His mother said to the servants, "Whatever He says to you, do it."*

~ JOHN 2:5

Father God, we need more faith
to simply obey Your commands,
just as the servants did when Jesus'
mother, Mary, told them to. They
filled the six waterpots of stone with
water and it turned into the finest
wine at the wedding in Cana.
Please help us to simply obey You
without any ifs, ands or buts.

— *Amen.* —

*The secret of a miracle is simple faith!*

# SERVANT OF GOD

*So the man of God said, "Where did it fall?" And he showed him the place. So he cut off a stick, and threw it in there; and he made the iron float.*

~ 2 KINGS 6:6

Father God, any one of us if asked
if an ax head could float on water
would say, "Absolutely not!" And yet
the man of God, Your servant Elisha,
because of his unwavering faith in You,
made it happen. Father, please use us
to glorify Your wonderful name too!

*Amen.*

*One genuine miracle equals
a thousand sermons!*

# FIRE FROM HEAVEN

*Elijah came to all the people, and said, "How long will you falter between two opinions? If the LORD is God, follow Him; but if Baal, follow him." But the people answered him not a word.*

~ 1 KINGS 18:21

Father, we ask forgiveness for so often being compromisers when it comes to standing up for You. We really need more people like Elijah, who feared no one but You. Please help us to be like Elijah, who was totally and absolutely dedicated to You alone.

 *Amen.*

*The fire only comes down when there is no doubt whatsoever.*

# INCREASED FAITH

*And the Scripture was fulfilled which says, "Abraham believed God, and it was accounted to him for righteousness." And he was called the friend of God.*

~ JAMES 2:23

Father God, You performed one of Your greatest miracles in the Bible when You gave Abraham a son, Isaac. Abraham was one hundred years old and Sarah was in her nineties. Yet You honored them because they believed in miracles! Please increase our faith, too, so that we also can trust You for a miracle.

— *Amen.* —

*A miracle would not be a miracle
if it could be explained.*
– J. C. Ryle

# ACKNOWLEDGE GOD

*This was the second miraculous sign Jesus did in
Galilee after coming from Judea.*

~ JOHN 4:54 NLT

Father God, Your Son Jesus is the
Miracle Worker. And He has not
changed in over two thousand years.
That is how the world acknowledges
that He is Your beloved Son;
not so much by what He says,
but rather by who He is. Holy Spirit,
please help us, Your children, to do
likewise for His honor and glory.

— *Amen.* —

*Jesus' life was a blaze of miracles.
Miracles were as natural to Him as they
would be unnatural to other men.*
– Karl Adam

# A HEART OF COMPASSION

*When Jesus saw him lying there, and knew that he already had been in that condition a long time, He said to him, "Do you want to be made well?"*

~ JOHN 5:6

Father God, what compassion we see in Jesus for sick and hurting people wherever He went! Please help us to have the same compassion for hurting and lost folk. For there are so many more people suffering now; we pray for more love and kindness for the whosoevers. Let Jesus' love and compassion shine through us.

*Amen.*

*The miracles were to the gospel as seals are to a writing.*

– William Gurnall

# FAITH IN GOD'S WORD

*God also bearing witness both with signs and wonders, with various miracles, and gifts of the Holy Spirit.*

~ HEBREWS 2:4

Father God, it is absolutely impossible to believe in Your Holy Word, the Bible, if we cannot believe in miracles. It is the absolute witness and proof that You are a miracle-working God. And we are so honored and excited to be witnesses for You.

*Amen.*

*Miracles must never be separated from the Word.*
– John Calvin

# GIFTS FROM THE SPIRIT

*He gives one person the power to perform miracles, and another the ability to prophesy. He gives someone else the ability to discern whether a message is from the Spirit of God or from another spirit.*

~ 1 Corinthians 12:10 NLT

Father, You are very clear through this passage of Scripture that You give out certain gifts to different people – just like the gift of the working of miracles. But the most important thing for us believers to remember is that all the different gifts come to us by the power of the Holy Spirit within us.

— *Amen.* —

*The chief means for attaining wisdom, and suitable gifts for the ministry, are the Holy Scriptures, and prayer.*
– John Newton

# A LIVING MIRACLE

*"When Pharaoh speaks to you, saying, 'Show a miracle for yourselves,' then you shall say to Aaron, 'Take your rod and cast it before Pharaoh, and let it become a serpent.'"*

~ Exodus 7:9

Father God, the world is still asking us, Your believing children, to show them a miracle just like Pharaoh asked Moses and Aaron. We pray that our lifestyles will be living miracles, so that folk will see lives that will draw them to You.

*Amen.*

*It is not the objective proof of God's existence that we want but the experience of God's presence. That is the miracle we are really after.*
– Frederick Beuchner

# FOCUS ON YOUR WORK

*But Jesus said, "Do not forbid him, for no one who works a miracle in My name can soon afterward speak evil of Me."*

~ MARK 9:39

Father, we see by this Scripture verse that there were, and still are, those who would perform miracles in Your name and yet still not follow You. And when the disciples tried to prevent them, You said to leave them. Father, we too shall concentrate on the work You've called us to do and leave the rest to You.

*Amen.*

*When we do the best that we can, we never know what miracle is wrought in our life, or in the life of another.*

– Helen Keller

# MIRACLES ARE POSSIBLE

*Marvelous things He did in the sight of their fathers, in the land of Egypt, in the field of Zoan.*

~ PSALM 78:12

Almighty God, You did such incredible
miracles in the midst of Your people –
like the parting of the Red Sea and
the water that gushed from the rock.
You sent a pillar of fire at night and
the cloud by day to direct Your nation
going through the wilderness. How can
we still doubt in Your miracle-working
power? Please remove all our doubts.

*Amen.*

*It is impossible on reasonable
grounds to disbelieve miracles.*
– Blaise Pascal

# BY FAITH ALONE

*Therefore He who supplies the Spirit to you and works miracles among you, does He do it by the works of the law, or by the hearing of faith?*

~ GALATIANS 3:5

Yes, Master, it is You alone, for no one else can perform miracles, signs and wonders. And it happens through faith and not by the law. Please increase our faith to believe, Lord Jesus, and that faith is only manifested through those of us who choose to follow after You fully.

 *Amen.*

*I never have any difficulty believing in miracles, since I experienced the miracle of a change in my own heart.*
– Saint Augustine

# DON'T BE DECEIVED

*Then the beast was captured, and with him the false prophet who worked signs in his presence, by which he deceived those who received the mark of the beast and those who worshiped his image.*

~ REVELATION 19:20

Lord Holy Spirit, please help us to discern between what is true and false, for there is just so much that is counterfeit in the world today. If we do not pray and seek Your divine counsel, we can also be duped into believing the false miracles performed by Satan. Please give us discernment and wisdom.

— *Amen.* —

*We must remember that
Satan has his miracles too.*
– John Calvin

# PATIENCE FOR DOUBTERS

*Although He had done so many signs before them,
they did not believe in Him.*

~ JOHN 12:37

It is just so terribly sad to see, Father,
that some folk will not believe!
Please give us, Your faithful ones,
more patience with those doubters,
because there was a time when
we, too, doubted. But not anymore,
Master, we believe You are
the miracle-working Son of
Almighty God. Hallelujah!

*Amen.*

*Men can see the greatest miracles and
miss the glory of God. What generation
was ever favored with miracles as
Jesus' generations was? Yet that
generation crucified the Son of God!*
– Tom Wells

# MIRACULOUS HEALING

*"What should we do with these men?" they asked each other. "We can't deny that they have performed a miraculous sign, and everybody in Jerusalem knows about it."*

~ ACTS 4:16 NLT

Father God, Peter and John
performed a miracle which no one,
not even their enemies, could deny.
We love You so much, for we know
also that no one, and nothing,
can perform such miracles as You can.
Please use us more, Lord, and give
us faith like Peter and John had.

*Amen.*

*Greater is He that is in us, than he
that is in the world (see 1 John 4:4).*

# GOD'S MIRACLES

*Gideon said to Him, "O my lord, if the Lord is with us, why then has all this happened to us? And where are all His miracles which our fathers told us about?"*

~ Judges 6:13

Father, even as Gideon had doubts, please forgive us, too, for sometimes wondering when our miracle will appear. We need You so very badly in these last days in which we are living and we ask You today to strengthen us for the battle, just like You did for Gideon.

— *Amen.* —

*God never wrought miracles to convince atheism, because His ordinary works convince it.*
– Francis Bacon

# A TRUE SIGN

*Then Gideon said to God, "Do not be angry with me, but let me speak just once more."*

~ Judges 6:39

Father, Gideon asked for a few signs that would convince him that You would be with him. We live in such a confused world these days, Father, and there is no one more trustworthy whom we can ask when we need to make very serious decisions in life. Please help us to trust You for the answers.

*Amen.*

*To strip Christianity of the supernatural is to destroy Christianity.*

– R. B. Kuiper

# SPEAK UP

*Sing to Him, sing psalms to Him; talk of all His wondrous works!*

~ 1 CHRONICLES 16:9

Father God, please forgive us for not speaking more about You and about all Your miracle-working power. This tired society in which we live is so desperately hungry for stories of Your great love and wonderful miracle-working power. Please give us more courage, Father, to speak up for You.

*Amen.*

*Miracles are a retelling in small letters of the very same story which is written across the whole world in letters too large for some of us to see.*
– C. S. Lewis

# COUNT YOUR BLESSINGS

*I will remember the works of the LORD; surely I will remember Your wonders of old.*

~ PSALM 77:11

Father God, sometimes it is so comforting and uplifting to remember the miracles of old that You have performed in our lives. Yes, to count our blessings and to name them one by one. You have done so many great works in our lives. Thank You, Father.

*Amen.*

*Count your blessings,*
*name them one by one;*
*count your many blessings,*
*see what God hath done.*
– Johnson Oatman

# A GOOD MEMORY

*"… His signs and His acts which He did in the midst of Egypt, to Pharaoh king of Egypt, and to all his land."*

~ DEUTERONOMY 11:3

Father God, when we have seen and heard of Your mighty miracles, signs and wonders, we have no excuse but to humbly obey Your written Word! Forgive us for so often forgetting Your marvelous deeds in the past. Help us not to be like the Israelites who so easily forgot Your miracles and blessings.

*Amen.*

*How quickly we forget God's great deliverances in our lives. How easily we take for granted the miracles He performed in our past.*
– David Wilkerson

# UNASHAMED

*"Jesus of Nazareth, a Man attested by God to you by miracles, wonders, and signs which God did through Him in your midst."*

~ ACTS 2:22

Father God, what power and anointing was displayed when Peter, under the unction of the Holy Spirit, preached. Approximately three thousand were added to the Kingdom that day. We will never apologize for the name of Jesus Christ. Please use us to spread the Good News to a suffering and dying world.

*Amen.*

*When a man is not ashamed of the gospel, then the power and anointing of God will support him!*

# REPUTATION COUNTS

*John performed no sign, but all the things that John spoke about this Man were true.*

~ JOHN 10:41

Father God, again we see the importance of reputation! Jesus had an amazing presence, so much so that everything John the Baptist said about Him came to pass, and even more. Our prayer, Father, is that our lifestyles will bring glory to our Lord Jesus. Please help us to be good ambassadors for You through our words and actions.

— *Amen.* —

*It's not so much what we say but rather who we are that impacts people's lives.*

# GOOD WITNESSES

*For this reason the people also met Him, because*
*they heard that He had done this sign.*

~ JOHN 12:18

Lord Jesus, the people flocked to
You because You performed a
great miracle by raising Lazarus
from the dead after four days.
There can be no doubt that You are
a miracle-working God when an
impossible thing like this takes place.
Help us to be good witnesses for
You by telling others about the
mighty things You have done.

*The Christian life itself is a miracle,*
*and every phase of it ought to bear*
*the mark of the supernatural.*
– Vance Havner

# CREATED TO BE UNIQUE

*God has appointed these in the church: first apostles, second prophets, third teachers, after that miracles, then gifts of healings, helps, administrations, varieties of tongues.*

~ 1 CORINTHIANS 12:28

Sweet Father, what we really love so much about You is that You have made us individuals. You have given to each of us different gifts and these are all integral parts of the body of Christ. Please help me to use my gifts for the benefit of the church and for Your glory.

— *Amen.* —

*All Christ's gifts are like Himself, spiritual and heavenly.*
– Thomas Brooks

# CONVINCED

*Then Simon himself also believed; and when he was baptized he continued with Philip, and was amazed, seeing the miracles and signs which were done.*

~ Acts 8:13

Father, it was the signs, wonders and miracles that convinced Simon the sorcerer to believe in the Lord Jesus. Simon was also baptized and followed Philip, convicted by his words and repenting of his sin. Lord, may we, too, be convinced and convicted as we read Your Holy Word and see what You have done.

*Amen.*

*It is wonderful what miracles God works in wills that are utterly surrendered to Him.*
– Hannah Whitall Smith

# ACTIONS SPEAK LOUDER

*And the multitudes with one accord heeded the things spoken by Philip, hearing and seeing the miracles which he did.*

~ ACTS 8:6

Heavenly Father, there is absolutely no doubt that a miracle speaks a thousand words, especially with people who have never experienced a living relationship with Your Son, Jesus Christ. We pray, dear Father, that You will equip us, Your children, with more faith to "walk upon the water", so that the lost might be saved.

— *Amen.*

*The same Jesus who turned water into wine can transform your home, your life, your family, and your future.*
– Adrian Rogers

# NOVEMBER
## *Amazing Grace*

# SUFFICIENT GRACE

*"My grace is sufficient for you, for My strength is made perfect in weakness." Therefore most gladly I will rather boast in my infirmities, that the power of Christ may rest upon me.*

~ 2 Corinthians 12:9

Father God, we love You unconditionally. Thank You for Your grace towards us. We praise You for the undeserved lovingkindness and unmerited favor You lavish upon us. Thank You for making us strong in our weakness.

 *Amen.*

*Anything this side of hell is pure grace.*

# UNDESERVED GRACE

*For by grace you have been saved through faith,*
*and that not of yourselves; it is the gift of God.*

~ EPHESIANS 2:8

Father, what a wonderful
reminder for us, Your children,
that our very faith and salvation
is of no doing of ourselves,
for it was a beautiful and totally
undeserved gift from You! All we,
Your undeserving children, can say
is a very grateful thank You, Master.

 *Amen.*

*Men may fall by sin but cannot rise up*
*themselves without the help of grace.*
– John Bunyan

# GOD-GIVEN GRACE

*The king loved Esther more than all the other women, and she obtained grace and favor in his sight more than all the virgins.*

*~ ESTHER 2:17*

Almighty God, we see that the
Jewish virgin Esther found extreme
favor from the king and we know
beyond any shadow of a doubt it was
because You gave her much grace
in the sight of the king. Even as Esther
used this favor to save her people,
please use us, Your children,
to exercise our God-given grace
and favor to do the same, we pray.

— *Amen.* —

*Every day we are objects
of the grace of God.*

# FULL OF GRACE

*Grace is poured upon Your lips; therefore God has blessed You forever.*

~ PSALM 45:2

Lord Jesus, how much do we,
Your people, love and adore You.
Truly, there is none like You.
And indeed, Your lips are so full
of grace towards Your people,
You are so kind. Please help us,
even today, to speak gracious
and gentle words to others.

*Amen.*

*The more grace thrives in the soul,
the more sin dies in the soul.*
– Thomas Brooks

# A LIGHT IN DARKNESS

*For the L*ORD *God is a sun and shield; the L*ORD *will give grace and glory; no good thing will He withhold from those who walk uprightly.*

~ PSALM 84:11

Father God, You are a Sun to us,
Your faithful children. But even more
than that, You gave us Your only
Son, Jesus! And He has become
to us, Your faithful children, a light in
the darkness. Help us today, please,
to shine as well wherever we might be.

*Amen.*

*Knowledge is but folly
unless it is guided by grace.*
– George Herbert

# AMAZING GRACE

*And the Child grew and became strong in spirit, filled with wisdom; and the grace of God was upon Him.*

~ Luke 2:40

Father, that same grace that Jesus was filled with has also been transferred upon each of us who believe. We think of one of the most famous of all hymns *Amazing Grace*, written by John Newton who was the captain of a hellish slave ship! And Your amazing grace, Father, touched and changed him instantly. Thank You for Your grace that saves wretched sinners.

*God does not owe you salvation. You deserve damnation, but He provides salvation.*
– Billy Sunday

# THE GIFT OF GRACE

*Because of our faith, Christ has brought us into this place of undeserved privilege where we now stand, and we confidently and joyfully look forward to sharing God's glory.*

~ ROMANS 5:2 NLT

Father God, please increase our faith so that we may be able to embrace Your grace even more, which You have made available to all those who follow You faithfully. Yes, we receive this wonderful gift of grace from You, Father, by faith. Thank You very much.

 *Amen.*

*They travel lightly whom God's grace carries.*
– Thomas à Kempis

# GRATEFUL FOR GRACE

*Let us therefore come boldly to the throne of grace,*
*that we may obtain mercy and find grace to help*
*in time of need.*

~ HEBREWS 4:16

Father, we come boldly into
Your presence, because of what
Your Son, our Savior, did for us on
Calvary. What incredible love we
have received. We do not deserve
to come before Your throne of grace
but we approach You for Your help
and mercy in this day. For which
we are eternally grateful, Master.

 *Amen.*

*Grace often grows strongest where*
*conviction of sin has pierced deepest.*
– Sinclair Ferguson

# GROW IN GRACE

*But grow in the grace and knowledge of our Lord and Savior Jesus Christ. To Him be the glory both now and forever.*

~ 2 Peter 3:18

Father God, we have been called to grow in grace. It is not a stationary thing, but it is alive and full of action. Help us to grow in grace and in our knowledge of our Savior. We intend, with Your help, to grow and become more effective for the Kingdom!

*Amen.*

*Grace is the freeness of love.*
– Thomas Goodwin

# SPIRIT OF GRACE

*"And I will pour on the house of David and on the inhabitants of Jerusalem the Spirit of grace and supplication."*

~ ZECHARIAH 12:10

Please, heavenly Father, do it again.
Pour out Your love and supplication
upon us, Your desperate people
who need You so very much
at present. We love You, Jesus,
and we could not contend one day
longer without You. Pour Your grace
upon us, Your children, we pray.

—— *Amen.* ——

*Grace is love that gives, that loves
the unlovely and the unlovable.*
– Oswald C. Hoffman

# HUMILITY LEADS TO GRACE

*The LORD curses the house of the wicked, but He blesses the home of the upright. The LORD mocks the mockers but is gracious to the humble.*

~ PROVERBS 3:33-34 NLT

Lord Jesus, You love the humble man or woman, and lavish Your grace upon them. But You have no time for the arrogant and proud person. We know only too well that pride always comes before a fall. Please help us to be upright and humble in Your sight.

*Amen.*

*The higher a man is in grace,*
*the lower he will be in his own esteem.*
– Charles Spurgeon

# PURE GRACE

*But we believe that through the grace of the Lord Jesus Christ we shall be saved.*

~ Acts 15:11

Father God, what beautiful words.
We know that through the unmerited
favor of Jesus Christ, pure grace,
we shall be saved. We do not
deserve it. We cannot pay for it.
We cannot even work for it. Freely we
have received and now freely we shall
give (see Matthew 10:8). Thank You
for Your grace that saves us.

*Amen.*

*Grace finds us beggars
but leaves us debtors.*
– Augustus Toplady

# BUILT UP IN GRACE

*I commend you to God and to the word of His grace, which is able to build you up and give you an inheritance among all those who are sanctified.*

~ Acts 20:32

---

Dearest Father God, what a beautiful Scripture verse. It's pure grace that is able to take a broken person and build them up again. Even this very day, please help us to build up those precious souls we come into contact with. Thank You for the inheritance we can receive through Your grace.

—— *Amen.* ——

---

*Grace is a universal principle.*
– William Gurnall

# A GRACE-FILLED LEADER

*Through Him we have received grace and apostle-ship for obedience to the faith among all nations for His name.*

~ ROMANS 1:5

---

Father, the role of leadership requires
much wisdom and much grace.
To be good servants for the people
and to be totally obedient to Your
call on our lives is not an easy thing;
it requires abundant grace.
Please help us to lead with the love
and kindness that You have shown us.

—— *Amen.* ——

---

*Any blessing which is bestowed by the
Father upon His undeserving children
must be considered to be an act of grace.*
– David Smith

# FREE GRACE

*Being justified freely by His grace through the redemption that is in Christ Jesus.*

~ ROMANS 3:24

O heavenly Father, we still cannot really grasp the enormity of Your free grace that You pour over us, Your children. We have been freely justified and redeemed through Your grace. Help us to please show much grace to our fellow man.

*Amen.*

*Behold, what wondrous grace the Father hath bestowed on sinners of a mortal race to call them sons of God.*
– Isaac Watts

# DRAW NEAR TO GOD

*Because of our faith, Christ has brought us into
this place of undeserved privilege where we now
stand, and we confidently and joyfully look forward to sharing God's glory.*

~ ROMANS 5:2 NLT

Father God, You have never
once denied us access into Your
wonderful presence! It is we,
Your children, who so often do not
exercise our faith to draw near to You.
Please forgive us. We, by faith, stand
on Your promises to us through Your
undeserved lovingkindness (grace).

*Amen.*

*The grace of God does not find men
fit for salvation, but makes them so.*
– Saint Augustine

# GRACE RECEIVED

*But to each one of us grace was given according to the measure of Christ's gift.*

~ EPHESIANS 4:7

Father God, You are such a wonderful
and caring Dad! Completely
impartial towards us, Your children.
Every single one of us receives grace,
but of course, how we receive it
is entirely up to us. We pray that
we shall by no means waste it.

— *Amen.*

*Common grace places everyone
continually in God's debt — and the
debt grows with every moment of life.*
– John Blanchard

# PARTAKERS OF GRACE

*… you all are partakers with me of grace.*
~ PHILIPPIANS 1:7

Lord Jesus, what an encouraging
statement made by Your faithful
servant Paul the apostle. We are
all partakers of the grace of God
(the unmerited favor of our God).
Of course, Paul wrote this verse
while in chains and we, too,
are ready to serve You, Master,
at whatever the cost.

— *Amen.* —

*Grace is the free favor of God; peace is the
condition which results from its reception.*
– H. L. Goudge

# SINGING WITH GRACE

*Let the word of Christ dwell in you richly in all wisdom, teaching and admonishing one another in psalms and hymns and spiritual songs, singing with grace in your hearts to the Lord.*

~ COLOSSIANS 3:16

Father God, we just love to sing
with grateful hearts to You for all
the kindness and goodness You
have given to us, Your children.
Grace is undeserved lovingkindness.
We do not deserve anything
from You, but because of Your
great love, we sing with gratitude.

 *Amen.*

*God gives His gifts where He finds the vessel empty enough to receive them.*
– C. S. Lewis

# RANSOMED BY GRACE

*Then He is gracious to him, and says, "Deliver him from going down to the Pit; I have found a ransom."*

~ JOB 33:24

Father God, we know the One who was ransomed for us, the Holy One who died for us, that we might live with You in paradise forever. His name is Jesus Christ, the Savior of the world. What a gracious God You are, Father, to send Jesus to show us the way to live and to lead us so that we do not fall into the pit.

— *Amen.* —

*The cross is the lightning rod of grace that short-circuits God's wrath to Christ so that only the light of His love remains for believers.*
– A. W. Tozer

# GOD'S MERCIFUL GRACE

*Has God forgotten to be gracious? Has He in anger shut up His tender mercies?*

~ PSALM 77:9

Father God, many a time You must grow so very despondent with us, Your rebellious children. Yet, once again, we thank You for Your Son, Jesus. Without His love, compassion and mercy we would not be here today. We know that You, Father, would never forget or shut up the mercies of Your love for us.

*Amen.*

*A Christian never lacks what he needs when he possesses in Christ the unsearchable riches of God's grace.*
– George Duncan

# STAYING FREE

*"Therefore if the Son makes you free, you shall be free indeed."*

~ JOHN 8:36

Lord Jesus, You have set us free
by Your wonderful grace that
never changes. But the thing that
holds us bound in chains more than
anything else is "self". Thank You
again, Master, for setting us free.
The best way to stay free is to love
others and deny ourselves.

*Amen.*

*Growth in grace is growth downward. It is
the forming of a lower estimate of ourselves. It
is a deepening realization of our nothingness.
It is a heartfelt recognition that we are not
worthy of the least of God's mercies.*
– A. W. Pink

# THE REAL JUDGE

*He is coming to judge the earth. With righteousness He shall judge the world, and the peoples with equity.*

~ Psalm 98:9

Father God, equity means to be judged with "the quality of being fair and impartial". That is exactly what You do, Father. We would never ever want to be judged by any other authority on earth. Your grace always abounds in mercy and fairness.

*Amen.*

*Grace is the very opposite of merit …*
*Grace is not only undeserved favor,*
*but it is favor, shown to the one*
*who has deserved the very opposite.*
– Harry Ironside

# THE GOOD NEWS

*"Whatever I tell you in the dark, speak in the light; and what you hear in the ear, preach on the housetops."*

~ MATTHEW 10:27

Lord Jesus, You have given to us, Your faithful children, the mandate, the holy order, to shout out the good news that there is salvation for all who believe in You. Thank You that You are able to save to the uttermost all those who come to You through faith in what You did on the cross for us.

 *Amen.*

*It's when we are not afraid to speak up in public that boldness and power is experienced.*

# THE GREATEST TEACHER

*The officers answered, "No man ever spoke like this Man!"*

~ JOHN 7:46

Father God, Your beloved Son, Jesus Christ, was undoubtedly the greatest orator that has ever walked the earth. A prolific public speaker, like no one had ever heard before, who told us about God's love and abundant grace. Please help us to walk with Him and obey His teachings.

— *Amen.* —

*Christ never said much in mere words about the Christian graces. He lived them, He was them. Yet we do not merely copy Him. We learn His art by living with Him.*
– Henry Drummond

# THE BREAD OF LIFE

*"I am the bread of life."*

~ John 6:48

> Beautiful words spoken for each and
> every one of us, Lord Jesus. The bread
> of Your living grace is sufficient food
> for each one of us, Your children.
> Lord, malnutrition is not only hunger
> and eventual starvation, but it is also
> not eating enough of the right foods.
> Please give us an appetite for
> Your Bible, the food of life itself.
>
> *Amen.*

*God gives us the ingredients for our daily
bread, but He expects us to do the baking!*

## LIVE LIKE JESUS

*A bruised reed He will not break, and smoking flax He will not quench; He will bring forth justice for truth.*

~ Isaiah 42:3

Father God, Your beloved Son, Jesus, has always led from the front! He has never asked any of us to do something that He has not done Himself before. The absolute gracious life He lived inspires us to imitate His selfless lifestyle. Being kind, gentle, loving and gracious is what we aspire to become.

*Amen.*

*If we give God service it must be because He gives us grace. We work for Him because He works in us.*
– Charles Spurgeon

# PRIORITIZE GOD

*Then He said to them, "What man is there among you who has one sheep, and if it falls into a pit on the Sabbath, will not lay hold of it and lift it out?"*
~ MATTHEW 12:11

Father God, we are so grateful that we are under grace and not under law. Our Lord's death on the cross and His resurrection changed everything. It is through Your grace that we can be made right and not through keeping laws. Help us not to be slow in showing grace to others too.

*Amen.*

*The law tells me how crooked I am.*
*Grace comes along and straightens me out.*
– Dwight Moody

# LOVE IN ACTION

*"Greater love has no one than this, than to lay down one's life for his friends."*

~ JOHN 15:13

Father God, this is surely an extreme example of (unmerited favor) grace. There is no more a person can give to his friend than to die for him. We, Your children, are lacking greatly in the area of expressing a life of grace by our lack of action. Please help us to be a channel of Your love and grace, not only receiving, but giving too.

— *Amen.* —

*A state of mind that sees God in everything is evidence of growth in grace and a thankful heart.*
– Charles Finney

# GENTLE WORDS

*You shall hide them in the secret place of Your presence from the plots of man; You shall keep them secretly in a pavilion from the strife of tongues.*

~ PSALM 31:20

Father God, please help us to manage our unruly tongues. To exercise grace when our carnal mind wants to retaliate with hurtful words when a person has said something ugly to us. Please help us not to retaliate, but to rather bring a kind and gentle word.

 *Amen.*

*Grace puts its hand on the boasting mouth and shuts it once for all.*
– Charles Spurgeon

# DECEMBER

*A Life of Service*

# SERVING OTHERS

*He poured water into a basin and began to wash the disciples' feet, and to wipe them with the towel with which He was girded.*

~ JOHN 13:5

Dearest Lord Jesus, what an amazing practical example and gesture for us to follow. If we are going to be Your faithful ambassadors here on earth, then we must serve each other in love and humility, showing this world, which is so selfish, that if we want to succeed then we must serve.

— *Amen.* —

*It is only because He became like us that we can become like Him.*

– Dietrich Bonhoeffer

# SERVE UNCONDITIONALLY

*So Moses arose with his assistant Joshua, and Moses went up to the mountain of God.*

~ EXODUS 24:13

Father God, what a great example Joshua is to us of a real serving heart. He remained faithful to his call to serve Moses right to the end. If we truly desire to be of use to You by any degree, we must be prepared to serve one another unconditionally.

*Amen.*

*As a servant of God, you must step back if the Lord is to reveal Himself through your service.*

– Basilea Schlink

# OF NO REPUTATION

*But made Himself of no reputation, taking the form of a bondservant, and coming in the likeness of men.*

~ PHILIPPIANS 2:7

Father God, if we are honestly going to serve You, we must ask You to please help us to put the flesh down. Every time we want to die to self, the evil one seems to come against us and tries to persuade us that we don't have to go this way to be a follower of Christ! Please help us to follow the example of the Master who made Himself a bondservant of no reputation.

*Amen.*

*It ill becomes the servant to seek to be rich, and great, and honored in that world where his Lord was poor, and mean, and despised.*
– George Müller

# A HUMBLE SERVANT

*"Most assuredly, I say to you, a servant is not greater than his master; nor is he who is sent greater than he who sent him."*

~ JOHN 13:16

Master, this Scripture verse contains a principle we are forever to remember. Yet, so often we forget that if it were not for Your love that pulled us out of the miry pit and gave us a second opportunity, we would still be there today. It is a humbling thing to be reminded of. Help us to serve You in humility.

*Amen.*

*The surrender to an implicit and unquestionable obedience must become the essential characteristic of our lives.*
– Andrew Murray

# BE THE LEAST

*Even though I am a free man with no master, I have become a slave to all people to bring many to Christ.*

~ 1 CORINTHIANS 9:19 NLT

Heavenly Father, this verse gives us a true example of self-denial. Paul, a free man, chose to be a servant to the least of all men in order that he might win more men for the gospel of Jesus Christ. Help us to do the very same, even today.

*Amen.*

*All divine work must be divinely initiated.*
– Watchman Nee

# CHOOSE GOD

*But Martha was distracted with much serving,
and she approached Him and said, "Lord, do You
not care that my sister has left me to serve alone?
Therefore tell her to help me."*

~ LUKE 10:40

Father God, there comes a time when
we need to listen and stop doing what
we are doing. Jesus gently cautioned
Martha and said that Mary had chosen
a better thing by stopping her work,
and listening to Him. Please help us
not to be so busy with Your work that
we don't spend time with You.

— *Amen.* —

*There is nothing in man that God
has not put there which may not
be employed in God's service.*
– Charles Spurgeon

# SERVING THE LORD

*... serving the Lord with all humility, with many tears and trials which happened to me by the plotting of the Jews.*

~ ACTS 20:19

Lord Jesus, serving can be a
dangerous and painful exercise
even to the point of death. You have
said before, Lord, that unless
we take up our cross and follow
after You, we cannot be called
Your disciples. We ask today for
more strength and courage to finish
the work You have called us to.

 *Amen.*

*You do not do God a favor by serving Him.*
*He honors you by allowing you to serve Him.*
– Victor Nyquist

# GIVE YOUR BEST

*Never be lazy, but work hard and serve the Lord enthusiastically.*

~ ROMANS 12:11 NLT

Almighty God, You are a
great and magnificent God.
Therefore when we, Your children,
serve You we need to realize that
we must be fervent and diligent.
We cannot afford to slack off and
work half-heartedly; we must be
willing to give our very best to You.

*Amen.*

*Love is the motive for working;*
*joy is the strength for working.*
– Andrew Bonar

# IN THE NAME OF GOD

*"And the King will answer and say to them, 'Assuredly, I say to you, inasmuch as you did it to one of the least of these My brethren, you did it to Me.'"*

~ MATTHEW 25:40

Father God, this Scripture verse is all we need to serve the very poorest of the poor. Because in so doing, we are serving You. Please help us, Holy Spirit, to be steadfast and to do an excellent job for our Master and Lord. Please help us to see You in every person who asks us to help them.

— *Amen.* —

*Whatever you do, begin with God.*
– Matthew Henry

# DO IT FOR JESUS

*God works in different ways, but it is the same
God who does the work in all of us.*

~ 1 CORINTHIANS 12:6 NLT

You have shown us, Father,
that there are different ways to
serve and sometimes preaching is
the very least effective. It is not just
about talking, it is about acting –
for example, it's very hard for a
hungry stomach to hear the Word
of God preached. Whether we be
farming, fishing, or baking to feed the
poor, we need to do it for You, Jesus!

— *Amen.* —

*There is nothing small in the service of God.*
– Saint Francis de Sales

# FREE TO SERVE

*"And you shall say to him, 'The LORD God of the Hebrews has sent me to you, saying, "Let My people go, that they may serve Me in the wilderness."'"*

~ EXODUS 7:16

Father God, in this very tired world
in which we are living at present,
there are many who are living
in captivity, just like the Israelites
of old. Please set us free so that we
can worship and serve You with
complete freedom and liberty.
Indeed, serving You brings tremendous
peace and joy to our hearts.

*Amen.*

*He is no Christian who does
not seek to serve his God.*
– Charles Spurgeon

# SERVE DILIGENTLY

*... made all who were present in Israel diligently serve the Lord their God. All his days they did not depart from following the Lord God of their fathers.*

~ 2 CHRONICLES 34:33

Father God, You must be so very proud of Your servant, the young King Josiah. He abolished all idols and instructed all Israel to serve You diligently. The young king obviously knew that we cannot serve two masters at once. And even we, Your unprofitable sons and daughters, desire to serve You with all our hearts.

— *Amen.* —

*Men who love much will work much.*

# I AM

*And God said to Moses, "I AM WHO I AM." And He said, "Thus you shall say to the children of Israel, 'I AM has sent me to you.'"*

~ EXODUS 3:14

Father, what an honor to serve You
as Your ambassadors. But we do
understand that with serving comes
a very grave responsibility. It took a
lot of courage for Moses to face the
people and they were not always
receptive. But You never left him
on his own, not once. Please be
with us and give us courage to do
what You have called us to do.

— *Amen.* —

*Strength for the strain is always
needed for service to the Lord.*

# MEETING JESUS

*Now when Herod saw Jesus, he was exceedingly glad; for he had desired for a long time to see Him, because he had heard many things about Him.*

~ LUKE 23:8

Dear Father God, without a doubt Your Son, Jesus, is the most popular Man who has ever walked on the face of the earth. Even the enemy was glad to meet Jesus! We, Your children, have an obligation to introduce Him to as many souls as we can while there is still time. Yes, it is our God-given service because when people meet Jesus, they are changed.

*Amen.*

*When we meet the Carpenter from Nazareth, we are changed forever.*

# LEADING GOD'S PEOPLE

*"Heaven and earth will pass away, but My words will by no means pass away."*

~ MARK 13:31

Father, You have given us a compass to lead people and to show them the way, the "Holy Bible". And just like You used Moses to lead the people of Israel through the wilderness for forty years, You are calling us to serve by leading lost souls into the Kingdom.

*Amen.*

*Find out where you can render more service, and then render it. The rest is up to the Lord.*

– S. S. Kresge

# A GREAT WORK

*As it is written: "Eye has not seen, nor ear heard, nor have entered into the heart of man the things which God has prepared for those who love Him."*

~ 1 CORINTHIANS 2:9

Father, You have such a great work prepared for those who are willing to serve You unconditionally. Help us, we pray, to expand our vision, to see the big picture and to believe for great service opportunities.

*Amen.*

*We are born into permanent service.*
– David Chilton

# LOOKING FORWARD

*But Jesus said to him, "No one, having put his hand to the plow, and looking back, is fit for the kingdom of God."*

~ LUKE 9:62

When serving You unconditionally, Father, we cannot possibly keep looking back. It is indeed the plowing principle. In other words, it is impossible to plow a straight line looking back to our past. Help us to remain focused on the future – eternal life with You.

*Amen.*

*When Jesus forgives, He forgets. Therefore, it is grossly unproductive to keep looking at our past.*

# AVOIDING DISTRACTIONS

*"I am doing a great work, so that I cannot come down. Why should the work cease while I leave it and go down to you?"*

~ NEHEMIAH 6:3

Father, when You call us to serve You,
it is a very important commitment.
We cannot allow ourselves to
become distracted, to be put off
of our service for You by people
who often have nothing else to do.
Please, Father, keep our eyes on You.

*Amen.*

*If you cannot be great, be willing
to serve God in that which is small.
If you cannot do great things for
Him, cheerfully do little ones.*

– S. F. Smith

# TRULY COMMITTED

*But without faith it is impossible to please Him,*
*for he who comes to God must believe that He is,*
*and that He is a rewarder of those who diligently*
*seek Him.*

~ HEBREWS 11:6

Father, it has been said that you
can't find honey if you are scared
of the bees. When we put our
hands up to serve You, we made
an unconditional commitment –
stings and all! Please help us to have
faith and to know that You will help us.

*Amen.*

*Better to have tried and failed*
*than to have never tried at all.*

# GOD WILL PROVIDE

*My God shall supply all your need according to His riches in glory by Christ Jesus.*

~ PHILIPPIANS 4:19

Father God, we don't need to beg, we only need to ask and You have promised us, Your sons and daughters, that we shall receive all our needs (not our wants) for the service of being Your hands and Your feet. Thank You for the riches we have in Christ Jesus!

*Amen.*

*If all the silver and gold belong to God, we have no need to ask anyone else for our daily needs.*

# SERVING ONE ANOTHER

*"These things I have spoken to you, that in Me you may have peace. In the world you will have tribulation; but be of good cheer, I have overcome the world."*

~ JOHN 16:33

Powerful words spoken by You,
Lord Jesus, for us, Your children.
Many people are stressed at present
with all the wars, sickness, poverty
and death everywhere. But this is
the believers' time to serve God
by serving one another. We ask,
Master, for more compassion, please.

— *Amen.* —

*Actions always speak louder than words.*

# GOD LOVES US

*"For God so loved the world that He gave His only begotten Son, that whoever believes in Him should not perish but have everlasting life."*

~ JOHN 3:16

Father, as always You lead us,
Your children, from the front.
The ultimate example of serving is
to be a doer and not just a talker.
You proved without a shadow of a
doubt that You love us by surrendering
Your precious Son, Jesus, so that
we might find eternal life. Help us
to show Your love to others.

— *Amen.* —

*We should be able to say, "Don't do what I say, rather do what I do!"*

# TURN THE OTHER CHEEK

*"But I tell you not to resist an evil person. But whoever slaps you on your right cheek, turn the other to him also."*

~ MATTHEW 5:39

Almighty God, this is a very hard Scripture verse to follow. We know it is not optional, if we love You then we must be prepared to serve You in all situations. It might mean turning the other cheek and even going the extra mile for someone who does not deserve it. Please Holy Spirit, give us that power we need!

— *Amen.* —

*I will go anywhere as long as it's forward.*
– David Livingstone

# TAKE UP YOUR CROSS

*"Whoever desires to come after Me, let him deny himself, and take up his cross, and follow Me."*

~ MARK 8:34

Heavenly Father, serving is all about dying to self, to put others above ourselves. But in doing so, we really start to live life to the full. In fact, the Bible tells us in 1 Timothy 6:6 that godliness with contentment is great gain. By living for You, Lord, and serving You, we have great joy.

—— *Amen.* ——

*Expect great things from God.*
*Attempt great things for God.*
– William Carey

# AMBASSADORS FOR GOD

*Now then, we are ambassadors for Christ, as*
*though God were pleading through us.*

~ 2 CORINTHIANS 5:20

Father, You have called us to serve
You and Your beloved Son as
representatives. Serving You, Lord,
in the marketplace of the world is
a very serious and most important
responsibility. We will watch
our words, lifestyle and actions
in order to make an honorable
impression to the world for You.

 *Amen.*

*We must take ourselves in hand,*
*and school ourselves, especially our wills,*
*into a greater fitness for the serious business*
*of being ambassadors of Jesus Christ.*
– Duncan Campbell

# OPEN YOUR EYES

*"Then a despised Samaritan came along, and when he saw the man, he felt compassion for him."*

~ LUKE 10:33 NLT

Father God, make us more observant.
Give us eyes to see the hurting,
the sick, the poor, the needy.
The Samaritan was not even a Jew,
yet he served the wounded man.
The Levite and the priest looked
the other way. Help us to
remember today that actions
speak much louder than words.

*Amen.*

*The gospel is not a doctrine
of the tongue, but of life.*
– John Calvin

# ETERNITY IN OUR HEARTS

*He has made everything beautiful in its time. Also He has put eternity in their hearts.*

~ ECCLESIASTES 3:11

Father, every man knows about eternity. You have put eternity in all of our hearts. We have a huge duty of service towards our fellow man. They need to be reminded that heaven is our home and not this tired old world. Thank You for making everything beautiful in its time.

— *Amen.* —

*Nothing below heaven is worth setting our hearts upon.*
– Richard Baxter

# THE LIVING GOD

*"For He is not the God of the dead but of the living, for all live to Him."*

~ LUKE 20:38

Heavenly Father, we just love this very powerful Scripture verse. To know beyond all shadow of a doubt that we serve a living God and not a dead historical figure is so uplifting and most exciting. And we look forward to seeing You soon in heaven, Father.

*Amen.*

*Heaven is not a state of mind.*
*Heaven is reality itself.*
– C. S. Lewis

# SET AN EXAMPLE

*Let every soul be subject to the governing author-ities. For there is no authority except from God, and the authorities that exist are appointed by God.*

~ ROMANS 13:1

Father, as Your voices in a world
that has absolutely no regard for
law and order, we need to set
an example. First and foremost,
we obey Your Word, then we need to
obey and serve the law of the land.
It is not optional; it must happen.

*Amen.*

*The law and the gospel are
allies, not enemies.*
– Walter Chantry

# BEING FRIENDLY

*A man who has friends must himself be friendly, but there is a friend who sticks closer than a brother.*

~ PROVERBS 18:24

Lord Jesus, You are our very best friend without a doubt. But if we, Your friends, are to do our part, then we also need to be friendly to other people. This is all part of serving. In fact, sometimes we need to be friendly especially to those who are unfriendly toward us.

*Amen.*

*A friend is one who comes in when the world has walked out.*

# BE OUTSPOKEN

*For I am not ashamed of the gospel of Christ, for it is the power of God to salvation for everyone who believes.*

~ ROMANS 1:16

Father God, there is no place in Your kingdom for a secret agent Christian. Please enable us, Your servants, to become more outspoken and not to withdraw when confronted about our faith. Help us to not be ashamed of the gospel because it is the power of God to save!

— *Amen.* —

*To call yourself a child of God is one thing. To be called a child of God by those who watch your life is another thing altogether.*
– Max Lucado